Student Workbook for Communicating for Managerial Effectiveness

Phillip G. Clampitt
Laurey Berk

SAGE Publications
International Educational and Professional Publisher
Newbury Park London New Delhi

For information:

 SAGE Publications, Inc.
2455 Teller Road
Thousand Oaks, California 91320
E-mail: order@sagepub.com

SAGE Publications Ltd.
6 Bonhill Street
London EC2A 4PU
United Kingdom

SAGE Publications India Pvt. Ltd.
M-32 Market
Greater Kailash I
New Delhi 110 048 India

Printed in the United States of America

Library of Congress Cataloging-in-Publication Data

Library of Congress Card No. 90-15581

ISBN 0-8039-5395-X

97 98 99 00 01 02 03   8 7 6 5 4 3 2

Sage Production Editor: Astrid Virding

Contents

Preface

Learning should be fun and challenging! That is why we developed this guidebook.
We want to encourage your further exploration of the complexities of organizational
communication. While we desire to facilitate your understanding of the concepts in
Communicating for Managerial Effectiveness, we also want to stimulate your thinking
about the subtle nature of communication in organizations.

For every chapter in *Communicating for Managerial Effectiveness* we have
provided a:

- Chapter Summary
- Set of Learning Objectives
- List of Key Terms and Concepts
- Chapter Outline

These are more traditional learning tools. But we also wanted to create some more
active learning tools that would stimulate both your mind and passions.   Therefore,
we designed three levels of exercises.

- **Knowledge:** These exercises are designed to ensure you understand key terms and
  concepts.

- **Analysis:** These exercises are more difficult. They ask you to analyze, explain, and
  further reflect on key notions discussed in the chapter. One feature in this section
  is the "thought quote" exercise in which we ask you to contemplate key ideas and
  record your own personal thoughts. While we suggest answers to these exercises,
  there are often many "right" answers that depend on your assumptions. When
  doing these exercises you might want to jot down your assumptions in the margin.

- **Synthesis:** These exercises are the most difficult. They require you to synthesize
  your knowledge by analyzing a situation in order to accomplish a communicative
  task. Most of the case studies are based on real incidents that pertain to the
  discussion in the chapter. As you progress through the book you will find that
  material from previous chapters can and should be incorporated into your case
  analysis. For example, in preparing your responses to a case in the information
  chapter you will find it helpful to use the principles discussed in the culture and
  communication chapters. When you get to the cases in Chapter 10, you should be
  able to see how concepts from all the previous chapters pertain to the analysis. This
  approach emphasizes the *integrative* nature of communication, showing, for

example, the interrelationships of fostering interdepartmental communication and creating and maintaining a spirit of innovation.

Your instructor can give you more guidance on how to proceed with the case studies but we can make several suggestions:

1. **You will have to make some "grounded assumptions."** A case can never provide all the nitty gritty details of a "live situation." Therefore, you will have to make some assumptions about the background. However, be cautious. Your assumptions should be "grounded" or based on a rationale. For example, if your case involves a bank, it would be inappropriate to assume that every employee had a college education. If demographic details are important to the case, then you would want to do some background research on the characteristics of bank employees. At that point you could convincingly argue that your assumptions were "grounded".

2. **Distinguish between the stated problems and the actual problems.** There may often be a conflict between what you, a communication expert, and the participants in the case perceive to be the primary issue. One of the critical objectives of these cases is for you to "tease out" the partially hidden issues.

3. **Clarify your communicative strategy.** Based on your problem analysis, you should be able to specify your general "plan of attack" for the case. What are the key communication objectives? For example, if you had to communicate a change, the strategic objectives might include:
   - Create a context for employees to understand the need for the change.
   - Legitimize employee fears about the change.

4. **Use the strategy to develop more specific tactics.** For example, you might develop an employee hotline to help employees cope with their fears. You would need to provide some details about how the hotline would function and how it would be publicized. You might develop a mock brochure for employees that explains background information about the change.

5. **Provide a rationale for your strategy and tactics.** The basic objective of the case work is to use the knowledge gleaned from the book to think through the situations. You need to be able to demonstrate the logical link between the case facts, problem analysis, strategy, and tactics. There are many ways to approach these cases. We suggest that you concentrate on the *thought process* you use to arrive at a solution rather than the "solution" itself. Concentrate more on providing a thorough rationale rather than a complete solution. In fact, it is not unusual for us to suggest that 60% of your efforts in case preparation should be devoted to the rationale and 40% to the "solution." By approaching a case in this manner, you will ultimately develop your own personal "thinking routine" for effectively dealing with communication problems. This is where meaningful learning takes place.

We hope you enjoy the guidebook. Have fun with the exercises! Experiment. Be creative. We believe these exercises will aid you in that never-ending quest to become an effective communicator!

Chapter 1: How Managers Communicate

Chapter Summary

This chapter presents three approaches to analyze managerial communication: the "arrow," "circuit," and "dance" approaches. The arrow manager tends to believe that "effective expression = effective communication" and views the receiver as a passive information processor. The circuit manager assumes that "understanding = effective communication." This manager believes that understanding will lead to agreement and that understanding should be the primary goal of communication. Both of these approaches simplify the communication process. A preferred approach is to use the "dance" metaphor, which expresses the nuances and complexity of organizational communication. There are many similarities of communication to dance. In both activities, there are patterns that emerge and rules, written or unwritten, that govern behavior .

Learning Objectives

After studying this chapter, you will be able to:

- describe the Arrow, Circuit, and Dance approaches to management

- identify behaviors of the above approaches

- identify strengths and weaknesses of the Arrow and Circuit approaches to management

- describe the similarities of communication to dance

- analyze a conversation and determine the regulative and interpretation rules

Key Terms and Concepts

arrow approach   p. 1-8
encoder   p. 6
decoder   p. 6
circuit approach   pp. 8-15
dance approach   pp. 15-23
coordination   pp. 16-17, p. 21
coorientation   p. 17

Chapter Outline

I. Arrow Approach
    A. How an arrow manager judges effectiveness
    B. How an arrow manager explains communication breakdowns
    C. Origins
        1. Technical training
        2. Speech teachers
        3. Personality predispositions
    D. Evaluation
        1. Weakness:
           Makes inappropriate assumption that effective expression = effective communication
        2. Strength:
           Encourages clear thought, specificity, accurate articulation

II. Circuit Approach
    A. How a circuit manager judges effectiveness
    B. How a circuit manager explains communication breakdowns
    C. Origins
        1. Human relations orientation to management study
        2. Interpersonal relations emphasis of some communication teachers
        3. Personality predispositions
    D. Evaluation
        1. Weaknesses:
           Makes inappropriate assumption that understanding = effective communication and that understanding is the goal of communication
        2. Strength:
           Emphasizes relational aspect of communication and feedback

III. Dance Approach
        Similarities of communication to dance
        1. Communication is used for multiple purposes
        2. Communication involves the coordination of meanings
        3. Communication involves coorientation

4. Communication is rule-governed
5. Communicators develop a repertoire of skills that may pass from the level of consciousness
6. Communication can be viewed as a patterned activity
7. The beauty of communication is a function of the degree of coordination

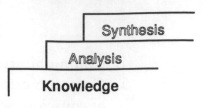

Exercise 1.1: Identifying the Type of Manager Orientation

What type of manager would most prefer the following words? Identify the Arrow Manager (A), Circuit Manager (C), and Dance Manager (D). Provide your rationale.

	<u>Word</u>	<u>Type of Manager</u>	<u>Rationale</u>
1.	understanding		
2.	performance		
3.	system		
4.	regulation		
5.	coordinating		
6.	give and take		
7.	command/order		
8.	procedures		
9.	connecting		
10.	coorienting		

Exercise 1.2: Identifying Regulative and Interpretation Rules

Label the following as a regulative rule (R) or interpretation rule (I).

Situation   Rule

1. If a person greets me, I return the greeting.

2. When someone insults me, I counter with an insult.

3. When someone says "they don't know," he or she is probably hiding something.

4. If someone says "are you sure?", he or she is questioning my personal integrity.

5. When my friend remarks, "that's very interesting," he really means the subject is uninteresting.

6. When my girlfriend says "it's fine," she really means it's average.

7. If someone tells a story about an event at work, I should tell a better story about the same subject.

Exercise 1.3: Identifying the Managerial Orientation

Synthesis
Analysis
Knowledge

What type of manager would most likely make the following comments? Identify the Arrow Manager (A), Circuit Manager (C), and Dance Manager (D).

1. "How can these people foul up this project ? I told them about it, I wrote a memo about how to do it and they still screwed up."

2. "What I value most about my managerial role is that people perceive me speaking with credibility and authority."

3. "I feel that my employees are most effective when they're open to one another and stress understanding and camaraderie."

4. "I know that some of my actions may not always be best for the interpersonal relationships at the plant, but I do believe that they are the best for the situation."

5. "Effective communicators have the ability to clearly and concisely put their thoughts into words."

6. "Effective communicators have the ability to understand their subordinates' concerns and are sensitive to how they can help them."

7. "I try to listen effectively to others so I can discern the 'real' wishes of those around me."

8. "Effective communicators recognize that each communication event is unique and try to communicate with each person in the context of that unique relationship."

9. "I try to know who I'm talking to and adapt my message accordingly."

10. "Effective communicators are aware of the interaction patterns between people so they adapt their messages as well as interpret them in light of these patterns."

Exercise 1.4: Thought Quote

Agnes De Mille made the following statement about Martha Graham, one of the greatest choreographers of all time. In the box below, discuss how this quote illuminates some ideas for students of the communication process.

> Painters, novelists, and of course actors have always known the meaning of expression instinctively. Acting, in fact, is the reproduction of these outer clues to inner feeling, and the more accurately these are reproduced, the more lively and effective the actor. The dancer, on the other hand, searches for the meaning behind the clues--he meanings behind gesture and expression--and then reassembles them, works them into a pattern, a design or purpose: in short, a conclusion. This is creative. This the great actor does also, but it is the essential stuff of choreography. (p. 22)
>
> --Agnes De Mille

Case 1.1: The Consulting Contract

Purpose: The purpose of this case is to learn how to communicate with different types of people while presenting a proper perspective on the nature of the communication process.

Situation: Your consulting team has been hired by a software design firm that employs 500 employees. Top management has determined that the 6 managers of the software development department and the 6 managers of the customer service department are "ineffective communicators." They have hired you to conduct a 2-hour introductory seminar on "Communicating for Managerial Effectiveness" for these managers. These managers have never participated in this kind of training and they are unaware that top management views them as "ineffective." All the managers have college degrees and are fairly young. The customer service managers have degrees in management and the software managers have degrees in computer science. Top management has told you that if this initial training is successful, they will hire your firm for a major contract. Your main contact is a young vice president who seems introspective. There are a number of paintings by Renee Magritte around the vice president's precisely organized room. Your initial meeting started and ended right on time.

Objectives:

1. Specify the precise material you would cover with each group of managers.

2. Specify how you would present the material.

3. Most important, provide a rationale for all your choices based on material discussed in the class and book.

Case 1.2: The MBA Class

Purpose: The purpose of this case is to learn how to communicate with different types of people while explaining the utility of knowing the difference between regulative and interpretation rules.

Situation: A professor of management read *Communicating for Managerial Effectiveness.* She knows you studied the concepts thoroughly and contacted you to teach a unit on communication for her MBA class. As you walk into her office, filled with uneven stacks of papers and books, you notice a variety of art books scattered about the office and a couple of Matisse posters askew on the walls. After you arrive, the professor jogs in carrying a book entitled *Leadership Jazz* by Max DePree. She says:

> I'm glad you came in today. Sorry I'm a bit late. I got caught up reading this book. It's great. Anyway, I know you are looking for a class project and I'm going to a convention in a month. I'd like you teach the communication unit to my MBA students. We meet for 3 hours on Wednesday night. I've read the *Communicating for Managerial Effectiveness* book and I think it's important to explain the ideas about Arrow, Circuit, and Dance managers. I like the ideas about communication rules but I guess I don't see how they apply to my students. I have 10 students who are mostly accountants in managerial positions. I had this idea that you could have a mock discussion between the three types of managers (Arrow, Circuit, and Dance) discussing a communication problem. It could be something simple, like how a manager should counsel an employee who is late for work several times. Then you could talk about the regulative and interpretation rules each was using during the conversation. Beyond this, I'm stuck. I want you to discuss with the class how knowing about these rules could be helpful in their jobs. Of course, the burden isn't completely on you. This mock interview should generate a lot of discussion. Feel free to suggest any other ideas. I've just highlighted the major content objectives for you. I'd like to meet with you in 3 weeks to see what you have in mind.

Objectives:
1. Specify the material you would cover in the class.
2. Determine how you would present the material to the class.
3. Specify how you would present your material to the professor.
4. Provide the rationale for each objective above.

Chapter 2: What Is Communication, Anyway?

Chapter Summary

This chapter presents 10 propositions about communication that provide a framework by which to judge the communication process. These propositions provide insight into what actually happens in the mind of the sender and receiver and why problems in communication occur. The propositions, such as that language is inherently ambiguous and that meaning construction is a product of the interaction of content and context, try to capture the highly fluid and dynamic nature of the communication process. Meanings are not simply the product of interpersonal relationships, but are influenced by a broader context of organizational rules, corporate environment, and culture.

What can managers do to facilitate this process? Managers must learn to think in terms of possible misinterpretations of their messages. In addition, the more they know about the context in which employees interpret messages, the greater the likelihood that they can accurately predict the probable interpretations.

Learning Objectives

After studying this chapter, you will be able to:

- identify and discuss several propositions of communication

- identify some implications of the propositions

- identify secondary messages in a conversation

- analyze a communication situation in terms of a "probability diagram"

Key Terms and Concepts

probabilities of communication interpretation   pp. 26-30
solidified interpretations/default assumptions   pp. 31-33
context/context construction   pp. 34-41
"black hole"   pp. 35-37
secondary messages   pp. 43-46
"blackout" tactic   p. 48

Chapter Outline

I. Propositions of communication
  A. Language is inherently ambiguous
  B. The communication process can be best described in terms of probabilities
      1. Typically the message sender sees only one possible interpretation
      2. The message sender may purposely use language that has multiple interpretations
      3. The receiver may purposely misunderstand
  C. Context can best be thought of as solidified interpretations--the default assumptions--that shape the probabilities
  D. A context is developed through the dynamic process of individuals interacting
  E. The context can become so powerful that it acts like a black hole
  F. Context construction is uniquely sensitive to time sequencing
  G. Meanings are a product of the interaction of content and context
  H. Meanings may be constructed without any message at all
  I. There are secondary messages in every communication event
  J. Even though interpretations are relative, the process of meaning construction is not

II. Implications of the propositions
  A. The more managers know about the context in which employees interpret actions and messages, the greater the likelihood that they can accurately predict the probably interpretations
  B. Managers must learn to think in terms of possible misinterpretations of their messages
  C. A useful strategy for facilitating understanding is to "block out" certain probable interpretations of a remark

Exercise 2.1: Identifying Key Communication Concepts

Which of the following statements about communication are consistent with the views expressed in Chapter 2? Check those that apply.

Statement	Consistent with Chapter 2?
1. context = situation	
2. meanings are shaped by context	
3. messages have one meaning	
4. context is internally generated by the individual	
5. what is not said is often as important as what is said	
6. probabilities rather than certainties govern the communication process	
7. the context is a highly stable enduring set of assumptions	
8. communication breakdowns are the receiver's fault	
9. communication breakdowns are the sender's fault	
10. taken-for-granted assumptions greatly influence meanings	

Exercise 2.2: Creating Probability Diagrams

Construct probability diagrams for the following terms. Then suggest a situational cue that would trigger a given probability. (Clearly you may not be able to plot all the probable interpretations. Try to plot the most likely.) For example, the word "hit" might be diagrammed as indicated below:

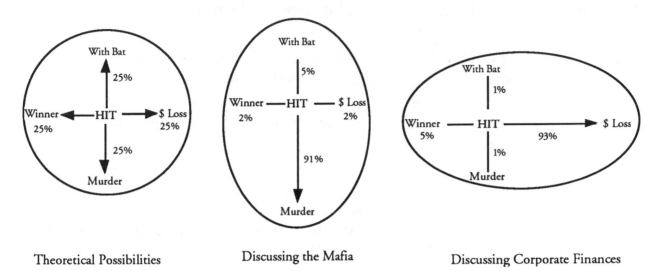

| Theoretical Possibilities | Discussing the Mafia | Discussing Corporate Finances |

A. Green

B. Max

C. Code

Exercise 2.3: Identifying "Default Assumptions"

In the following situations: (1) describe three probable "default assumptions" held by the participants that provide meaning for the comments and (2) discuss the reason those assumptions are held. Recall that a "default assumption" is something you "either consciously or unconsciously believe is implied" by the context. For example, default assumptions can deal with the following issues: subject matter, time frame, and the interpersonal relationship between the communicators.

A. In the Professor's office a student asks the teacher, "How am I doing?"
   - ex. The subject matter involves classroom performance.

   - ex: The professor is in a position to know about the student's level of performance.

   -

B. As an employee and supervisor study the department's monthly sales figures, the employee asks her boss, "How am I doing?"
   -

   -

   -

C. At an after-work office party, a supervisor asks her employee, "How am I doing?"
   -

   -

   -

D. At a back-to-school "mixer," a boyfriend asks his girlfriend, "How am I doing?"
   -

   -

   -

Exercise 2.4: Identifying Primary and Secondary Messages

Almost every comment has certain secondary messages. List the primary message and two probable secondary messages implicit in the following comments.

1. At a serendipitous meeting in a local restaurant the following introduction was made: "Phil, I'd like to introduce you to Dr. and Mrs. Snodpillar. Dr. Snodpillar is a prominent proctologist in Chicago. (handshake) Phil teaches at a local university."

    Primary message
    •

    Secondary message
    •

    •

2. A presidential candidate remarks to a minority group: "Now what you people need is economic opportunity, not handouts."

    Primary message
    •

    Secondary message
    •

    •

3. A manager receives the following written notice from the CEO along with his copy of the company's monthly report: "The results of a recent communication assessment have suggested that we cut back on the distribution of this monthly report. Therefore, your name will be removed from the monthly report distribution list after this issue."

    Primary message
    •

    Secondary message
    •

    •

Exercise 2.5: Thought Quote

John Wheeler was the physicist who coined the term "black hole." In the following quotation he tries to describe the phenomena. In the box below, describe a situation that has a similar pattern.

Friends ask me, "What if a black hole is black? How can you see it?" And I say, have you ever been to a ball? Have you ever watched the young men dressed in their black tuxedos and the girls in their white dresses whirling around, held in each other's arms, and the lights turned low? And all you can see is the girls. Well, the girl is the ordinary star and the boy is the black hole. You can't see the black hole any more than you can see the boy. But the girl going around gives you convincing evidence that there must be something there holding her in orbit. (p. 85)

--J. Wheeler

Case 2.1: The "Communication President"

Synthesis

Analysis

Knowledge

Purpose: The purpose of this case study is to develop a deeper understanding of how the communication process operates in an organizational context.

Situation: A grocery store chain recently appointed a new president. You are the communication specialist in the organization, which has 18 departments and 350 employees. The second day on the job, the president called you into her office, where a picture of T.S. Eliot was prominently displayed among a disarray of papers and files. She warmly greeted you and said that she wanted to "kick around a few ideas." She told you that she wants to be known as the "Communication President." She wants you to devise a "talking proclamation . . . kind of like the Ten Commandments, my Magna Carta," for the employees that demonstrates her commitment to effective communication. She relayed the following:

Here's my idea. I want everyone to feel free to discuss anything with me or anyone else. I would like to foster an open climate here. I'd like to draft a statement of my communication principles. For instance, we could say something like: "Effective communication is the basis for an effective organization." No, I like this better: "I believe effective communication is the basis for an effective organization." You get the idea? Then we could list some principles like:

- My door is always open.
- Communication should always be frank.
- Keep all employees appraised of relevant information.
- Address everyone by his or her first name.
- Make sure you thoroughly understand someone before criticizing his or her ideas.
- Always listen first, talk second.
- Even if you think you understand someone, check to make sure.
- Be sensitive to others.
- Be open to new ideas.

That should give you a feel for what I'm trying to do. Since you are the communication expert, you can revise these ideas and get back to me with a specific proposal.

Objectives:
1. Specify the precise proposal you would make to the president.
2. Specify the approach you would use in presenting the proposal.
3. Provide the rationale for the approach and proposal.

Case 2.2: Report to the Board

Purpose: The purpose of this case is learn how to present a message that effectively manages the probabilities of the communication process.

Situation: You are the newly appointed "communication advisor" to the president of a large local bank with 15 branch offices. You are in charge of both internal and external communications. From time to time you are asked to advise the president on major speeches. The president is a serious cerebral person who is risk averse. He runs a very conservative operation. He did not allow the bank to get into any risky investments during the 1980s and felt vindicated when other financial institutions suffered a subsequent erosion in credibility. He runs the bank with a precision, dedication, and attentiveness to detail that is legendary. His sole luxury is a 35-foot sailboat that he escapes to on weekends with his family.

The problem is that he has to make a major presentation to the board next month. This will be the third straight year the bank has not made its projected financial goals. In previous years he argued that the results were an aberration. Why this is continuing to happen is a bit unclear. There are a few new (but not serious) competitors and growth in the region, while not great, remained steady. He is frustrated about pinpointing the exact cause or causes of the problem. He sent you a memo (see next page).

In the back of his mind is a serious concern about his credibility. What advice would you give?

Objectives
1. Specify how you would answer his query.
2. Provide a rough outline of the two speeches.
3. How would you present your suggestions to the president?
4. Characterize the situation in terms of the ideas discussed in Chapter 2.
5. Provide a thorough rationale for your strategic and tactical recommendations.

To: Communication Director
From: President

I'm scheduled to make two major addresses next month. We have not achieved the financial results I expected. First, I must explain that to the board. Please advise on the following issues:

- When should I distribute the written documentation for the board meeting?
- What should be the content of the documentation?
- When in the presentation should I bring up the financial results? In addition, I'll be addressing the following issues in the presentation: Plans for future expansion, progress with ongoing projects, current economic pressures in our region, competitive pressures, and progress on our organization's corporate values.
- How should I handle questions in regard to falling short of our financial goals?
- What are my options for explaining the situation?
- What sort of proof (examples, statistics, graphs) should I use in the presentation?

Second, I'm scheduled to give the annual "State of the Bank" speech to our employees the week after the board meeting. Should this speech be handled differently (see questions above)? I've always freely shared information with employees about how the bank is doing. I'm wondering if this is the time and place to encourage employees to make suggestions about how to improve our financial situation.

Chapter 3: Communicating the Corporate Culture

Chapter Summary

Every organization, just like every society, has a culture that defines its essence. Corporate culture consists of the fundamental value and belief structure of the organization collectively shared by the employees that is symbolically expressed in a variety of overt and subtle ways. The type of people in the organization as well as the corporate symbols, slogans, and philosophies are all clues into corporate values.

Corporate culture influences the organization in a number of ways. It influences how an organization analyzes and solves problems as well as how the company responds to change. It also impacts the quantity and quality of innovations developed by the organization.

The I-We-Them-It Principle provides insight into an organization's culture. The "I" theme refers to the relationship of the individual to the corporation; in other words, the kind of people that are valued by the corporation. The "We" theme addresses how individuals relate to one another. The "Them" theme refers to how the corporate culture deals with the business environment, particularly the customer. The "It" theme represents how the organization feels about what it does. How do managers instill these values? They construct cultural cues for their employees whenever possible by (1) using the socialization process of a new employee to communicate the corporate culture, (2) linking values with specific behaviors, and (3) investing their financial resources in projects to communicate corporate values.

Learning Objectives

After studying this chapter, you will be able to:

- define culture

- describe why organizations have culture and how their values can be discovered

- discuss the consequences of culture

- describe the various cultural relationships that exist in the organization (the I-We-Them-It principle)

- identify how an organization communicates its values

Key Terms and Concepts

culture   p. 51
I-We-Them-It principle   pp. 62-64
corporate symbols   p. 55
corporate values   pp. 53-56
corporate socialization   p. 65
safety valves   p. 70

Chapter Outline

I. What is culture?

II. Why do organizations have culture?
   A. Culture identifies ideas and beliefs by which to live
   B. Culture provides a mechanism to coordinate the activities of employees
   C. Culture allows workers to be self-motivated by a set of internalized beliefs
       and values

III. How can the values be discovered?
   A. Type of people in the organization
   B. Corporate symbols
   C. Corporate slogans
   D. Corporate philosophies
   E. Other subtle indicators

IV. What are the consequences of culture?
   A. Influences how an organization analyzes and solves problems
   B. Impacts the quantity and quality of innovations in the company
   C. Influences how the company will respond to change
   D. Impacts employee motivation

V. The I-We-Them-It principle
   A. "I" theme: expresses the relationship of the individual to the
       organization
   B. "We" theme: expresses how individuals relate to one another in the
       organization
   C. "Them" theme: expresses how the corporate culture deals with the
       business environment

D. "It" theme: expresses how the organization feels about what it does

VI. How the organization communicates its values
   A. Through the socialization process of employees
   B. Through its symbols
   C. By linking values with specific behaviors
   D. By reconciling the inevitable conflicts between values
   E. By analyzing how it invests its financial resources
   F. By studying how new values evolve

Exercise 3.1: Identifying the I-We-Them-It Theme

What theme (I, We, Them, It) is demonstrated in the following corporate practices? Provide your rationale.

a. A company president insists that every employee be called an "associate."

b. A company provides special parking privileges for the "employee of the month."

c. A number of employees complain to a supervisor about the quality of raw materials. The response: there's no time to order new materials--there are production deadlines to meet.

d. In a prominent position in a real estate office is a board ranking every agent's sales production.

e. When an employee confronts a manager about a small defect in a product, the manager responds by saying, "We have to meet the deadline, no one will notice."

f. A customer complains about an overcharge on a meal because the waiter misunderstood the order. The manager apologizes for the misunderstanding but keeps the charge on the bill.

g. On a daily basis, a rug manufacturer monitors over 100 different "quality indicators" during the manufacturing process. However, the company only monitors customer complaints on a yearly basis.

Exercise 3.2: Interpreting Organizational Missions

a. Steven Jobs's mission statement for Apple Computer was to "make a contribution to this world by making tools for the mind that advance humankind." List three reasons why this is a better mission than "to be the best personal computer maker in the world."

-

-

-

b. Merck is considered one of the world's most innovative and successful pharmaceutical companies. Its purpose is "preserving and improving human life." List three reasons why this is a better mission than "to become a world-class developer of pharmaceutical products."

-

-

-

24

Exercise 3.3: Identifying the I-We-Them-It Theme With the Managerial Orientation

In the chart below indicate the values each type of manager is likely to encourage in his or her organization.

	Arrow	Circuit	Dance
I	• Only the tough survive		
We		• Everyone is treated equally	
Them			
It			

Exercise 3.4: Thought Quote

David Armstrong is a vice president of Armstrong International, a manufacturer with offices throughout the world. His book, *Managing by Storying Around: A New Method of Leadership*, advocates the use of stories to manage the workplace. Clearly this creates a unique corporate culture that differs greatly from most corporations. The thought quote below states Armstrong's philosophy. What are your reactions to using stories as the primary management tool? What strengths and weaknesses do you find in this approach?

> We have found stories so effective, they've replaced our policy manual. . . .
> Storytelling is a much simpler and more effective way to manage. I don't have to make thousands of individual decisions--is it okay to have a drink with dinner? how about charging an in-room movie to the hotel bill?--about what can or cannot go on someone's T&E report. The story gives people our guidelines, and then it is up to them. Storytelling promotes self-management. (p. 11)
>
> --David Armstrong

Case 3.1: Detecting Corporate Culture

Purpose: The purpose of this case study is to analyze the impact of organizations' cultural values on communication patterns.

Methods:

1. Select two companies to compare and contrast.

2. Collect various "artifacts" (slogans, corporate philosophy, etc.) that are representative of the culture.

3. Conduct interviews with various employees to determine corporate heroes, stories, and values.

4. Determine two or three critical values of each company that are suggested by your research.

5. Provide specific evidence from your research that backs up your selection of the values.

Objectives:

1. Discuss how the values are communicated in the company and how the values interact with one another.

2. Determine the likely communication strengths and weaknesses of the companies based on the above analyses and your knowledge of organizational communication. Provide sufficient rationale for your speculations.

3. Speculate on the "health" of each culture.

4. Compare and contrast the cultures of the two companies.

5. Summarize what the exercise has taught you about communication and corporate cultures.

Case 3.2: Serving the Community

Purpose: Develop tactics for strategically implementing a new corporate culture.

Situation: A successful businesswoman has just purchased a chain of fast food restaurants. For the past 5 years she was a highly successful real estate salesperson. Her colleagues thought her purchase of the 10 restaurants was rather odd. The businesses have shown only modest profits over the years. She believes that there is greater potential than has been realized. After all, the restaurants are located in prime locations. She called you to ask for some advice. As you walk into her spacious office filled with plaques commemorating her community service and accomplishments, she explains:

> I know I could continue to be successful at real estate but I wanted a new challenge. To be frank, I was bored with the routine. I read that something like half of all workers in the year 2000 will have worked at a fast food restaurant at one time or another. This is where young people learn about the work world, they become socialized in this industry. I want to give something back to the community. This doesn't sound glamorous but I view it as an opportunity to influence the next generation.

> One of the challenges is to develop a "culture of excellence." I've read Peters and Waterman (*In Search of Excellence*) and all the gurus about corporate culture. Their ideas make a lot of intuitive sense to me. I'd like to find a way to implement them. Part of my problem is that much of the culture derives from a very centralized home office. I don't want to take dictates from a corporate office I rarely see. I want to make a difference in these young peoples' lives. What I'd like is a game plan with specific actions that I could use to establish a "culture of excellence." The business is not even close to its potential. I want all employees, from managers to order-takers, to believe in the primacy of "customer service." Right now we operate like a giant vending machine with "customers" pulling the levers and the employees acting like the gears in the machine. How does one communicate a change in culture explicitly and implicitly?

Objectives:
1. Determine a communication strategy for the new owner.
2. Develop a list of ten specific acts or programs for the implementation of the strategy. Provide specific examples.
3. Determine how you would present the material to the owner.
4. Provide the rationale for each objective.

Chapter 4: Information

Chapter Summary

Traditional definitions of organizational excellence that emphasize the effective management of people and tasks omit an important dimension: the management of information. Today's greatest challenge facing managers may well be how to convert the bountiful quantity of data available to useful information that provides empowerment to the organizational members.

The organization can more clearly deal with information concerns by categorizing information along two dimensions: the availability of information (is it known or unknown?) and its "processing" state (has it been processed or consumed?). This approach generates four perspectives that each have unique challenges for the manager.

Information management also deals with reconciling conflicting forces, such as how to deal with the massive quantities of information that inundate most organizations (overload vs. underload), how to time the information (today vs. tomorrow), and determining if information should be open to all or available on a "need-to-know" basis.

To address this challenge, several principles are noted that guide the development of a sound information management system. Realizing that "the form the information takes can be as important as the substance" and that "who sends the information and from where it originates may be as important as the substance" generates some useful tactics to meet the challenge. The organization may decide to (1) conduct a thorough information analysis that provides an in-depth look at how information is disseminated, (2) realign information priorities to ensure that information needs are met, or (3) develop a communication policy that ensures that the system is flexible enough to deal with novel situations but rigid enough to discourage communication that puts redundant demands on people.

Learning Objectives

After studying this chapter, you will be able to:

- discuss myths about information

- identify the four "perspectives" on information and their implications

- recognize tension points in information management

- identify strategic principles that guide the development of a sound information management system

- discuss useful tactics that improve an information dissemination system

- identify employee interest levels in various types of organizational information

Key Terms and Concepts

Chapter Outline

I. Myths
   A. Information is a commodity
   B. Information is power
   C. More information is better
   D. Information is value-free
   E. Information is knowledge

II. Perspectives on information: questions addressed
   What information is available?
   Has the information been processed?
   A. Processed information
      Information that is available and has been "processed"
   B. Unprocessed information
      Information that is available but has not been "processed/consumed"
   C. Knowledgeable ignorance
      Awareness that information is needed but not currently available

D. Absolute ignorance
   Unawareness that pertinent information exists
E. Implications
   1. Each perspective suggests a unique challenges for the manager
   2. Information management must always be viewed from the perspective of the individual or department
   3. There are second-order concerns implied by this approach to information management, such as the proper mix of strategies to cope with information

III. Tension points: conflicting forces in information management
   A. Timing of information: "Today vs. tomorrow"
   B. Quantity of information: Overload vs. underload
   C. Availability of information: "This and that"
   D. Networking of information: Formal vs. informal
   E. Direction of information through the hierarchy: "Up vs. down"
   F. Reliance on evidence and theory: "Fact vs. theory"
      1. Evidence inherently reflects a bias
      2. A good theory has a simplicity and elegance about it
   G. Form of information: "Hard vs. soft"

IV. Strategic principles
   A. The more links in the communication chain, the more likely that information passed along the chain will be distorted
   B. The form the information assumes can be as important as the substance
   C. Who sends the information and where it originates may be as important as the substance
   D. The way information is organized can significantly alter its meaning
   E. The quality of the information decreases as the focus reaches beyond past experiences
   F. A variety of factors impact an individual's information load

V. Useful tactics
   A. Work on the details
   B. Realign information priorities
   C. Develop special training programs
   D. Conduct a thorough information analysis
   E. Discover and resolve problematic cycles
   F. Develop a communication policy

Exercise 4.1: Employee Interests in Organizational Information

Synthesis

Analysis

Knowledge

Employees have a wide range of interests in a variety of organizational topics. Rank the following subjects according to interest level. Rank 1 = highest, Rank 5 = lowest.

_____ a. Personal news (birthdays, anniversaries etc.)

_____ b. Corporate financial results

_____ c. Organizational plans for the future

_____ d. Personnel changes and promotions

_____ e. Personnel policies and practices

Exercise 4.2: Information Source Preferences

Although employees receive information from a wide variety of sources, they have preferences for their sources. Rank the following sources according to employee preference. Rank 1 = highest, Rank 5 = lowest.

_____ a. Grapevine

_____ b. Immediate supervisor

_____ c. Top executives

_____ d. Local employee publication

_____ e. Bulletin boards

Exercise 4.3: Providing Perspective on Information Problems

This chapter presented four concepts that are central to effective information management: Processed Information (PI), Unprocessed Information (UI), Knowledgeable Ignorance (KI), and Absolute Ignorance (AI). Which concept is most strongly related to the following information problems?

_____ 1. Information overload.

_____ 2. Employees claim that corporate documentation contains overly technical jargon.

_____ 3. The training department, in consultation with the engineering department, lays out training objectives for the company in order to insure key employees are fully informed on the latest technology.

_____ 4. A company sets up a "sabbatical program" so that researchers who have worked with the company 7 years or more can take up to 6 months off and investigate anything they want to. The "wackier," the better.

_____ 5. A defense manufacturing company has such cumbersome security clearances that many employees simply "give up" and operate in the dark.

_____ 6. A bicycle company goes into bankruptcy because it reacted too slowly to the mountain bike craze. The corporate executive said, "I didn't know what a mountain bike was until it was too late."

_____ 7. Information underload.

_____ 8. The plant manager of a paper mill claims that employees are overly obsessed with the number of tons of paper produced every day. They tend to judge their performance solely on this figure.

Exercise 4.4: Communication Cycles

The author has often used the following diagram to explain the relationship between data, information, knowledge, and empowerment.

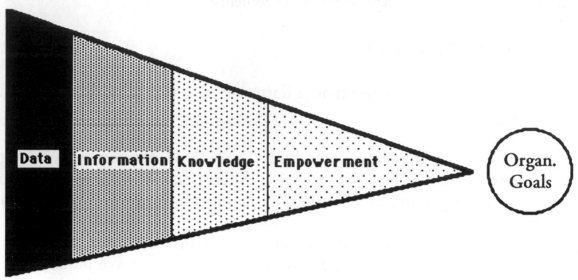

How would you distinguish these key terms?

    Data:

    Information:

    Knowledge:

    Empowerment:

What are three advantages of displaying these concepts in this format? (Hint: Look at the visual choices implicit in the diagram)

- •
- •
- •

What are two weaknesses of this format?
- •
- •

Exercise 4.5: Thought Quote

The English philosopher Mary Midgley is intrigued by the relationship between information, wisdom, wonder and knowledge. In the quote below she discusses one of the central paradoxes about our "information age." What is paradoxical about the skill she describes? What evidence do you find in the business world that we need this skill? What are the consequences of **not** having it? How would you know if someone had this skill?

> ... learning 'how to live without certainty and yet without being paralysed by hesitation' is indeed a most necessary skill for our lives. And this skill gets more crucial as more and more information is continually being flung at us. (p. 117)
>
> --M. Midgley

Case 4.1: Information Display

Purpose: Learn how to display information effectively to a specific audience.

Situation: You are a member of a task force that has been asked to revise your university's timetable of course offerings. Your goal is to make the timetable more useful to students. The recommendations will be forwarded to the Chancellor.

Objectives:
1. Develop a sample of how the new timetable should be laid out.
2. Determine a strategy for presenting your ideas to the Chancellor.
3. Provide the rationale for each objective.

Case 4.2: Managing Information Flows

Purpose: Learn how to manage information effectively.

Situation: You are hired by your local library to develop a specific "communication device" that will teach freshman how to write a term paper in order that they may fully utilize the resources available at the University.

Objectives:
1. Specify the precise proposal you would make to the library staff.
2. Specify the approach you would use in presenting the proposal.
3. Provide the rationale for the approach and proposal.

Chapter 5: Communication Channels

Chapter Summary

The number of communication channels available to the average manager has mushroomed over the last 20 years. Video tapes, audio tapes, electronic bulletin boards, fax machines, and teleconferences are just a few of the new possibilities. Every channel has unique nuances that can hinder or improve the effectiveness of the manager. One of the greatest challenges for today's managers is how to manage effectively the myriad of communication channels that are available.

The major criterion used in channel selection is personal convenience. As a channel's ease of use increases, so does the likelihood of its use. Little consideration is given to how the channels filter the message as well as the secondary messages the channel generates.

One approach to selecting a channel is based on a simple model of communication and considers four elements:
- *the needs of the sender*
- *the attributes of the message*
- *the attributes of the channel*
- *the needs of the receiver*

By addressing these factors, the choice of communication channel will be a product of skill and insight rather than chance. Wise managers realize that the choice of channel for their messages can make the difference between effective and ineffective communication.

Learning Objectives

After studying this chapter you will be able to:

- discuss various myths of disseminating information

- describe the various channel alternatives available

- evaluate the various channels according to various comparison criteria

- determine how to select the appropriate channel

Key Terms and Concepts

Chapter Outline

I. Myths of disseminating information
   A. More communication = better communication
   B. Written communication = fulfilled obligation
   C. Informing = persuading
   D. One channel = efficiency
   E. Channel proliferation = increased informativeness

II. Channel alternatives
   A. Face-to-face
   B. Telephone
   C. Group meetings
   D. Formal presentations
   E. Memos
   F. Mail
   G. Fax
   H. Employee publications
   I. Bulletin boards
   J. Publications
   K. Audio- and videotapes
   L. Hotlines
   M. E-mail
   N. Computer conferencing
   O. Voice mail
   P. Teleconference

Q. Video conference

III. Channel comparison criteria
    A. Feedback potential
    B. Complexity capacity
    C. Breadth potential
    D. Confidentiality
    E. Encoding ease
    F. Decoding ease
    G. Time-space constraint
    H. Cost
    I. Interpersonal warmth
    J. Formality
    K. Scanability
    L. Time of consumption

IV. Considerations for selecting the appropriate channel
    A. Are the sender's needs compatible with the attributes of the intended message?
    B. Are the messages compatible with the channels used?
    C. Are the sender's needs compatible with the type of channels used?
    D. Are the messages compatible with the receiver's needs?
    E. Are the receiver's needs compatible with the channels used?

Exercise 5.1: Rating Feedback Potential of Channels

Rank the following channels according to feedback potential. Rank 1 = highest, Rank 5 = lowest. Provide your rationale.

_____ Teleconference

_____ E-mail

_____ Face-to-face

_____ Fax

_____ Memo

Exercise 5.2: Rating Encoding Ability of Channels

Rank the following channels according to the ability to effectively encode complex messages. Rank 1 = highest, Rank 5 = lowest. Provide your rationale.

_____ Telephone

_____ Video conference

_____ Bulletin boards

_____ Computer conference

_____ Face-to-face

Exercise 5.3: Selecting Appropriate Channels

For the following situations select a communication channel that would be (a) most useful and (b) one that would be least useful. Provide your rationale.

1. A manager wants to persuade the 15 employees of her department about the merits of a new bonus plan being implemented by the company.

    a.

    b.

2. A manager wants to schedule a meeting of his 10 traveling salespersons.

    a.

    b.

3. An employee wants to recruit members for the company softball team.

    a.

    b.

4. The company wants to distribute information about its financial performance to employees on a regular basis.

    a.

    b.

5. A professor wants to disseminate advising information effectively to students.

    a.

    b.

Exercise 5.4: Thought Quote

Arnound De Meyer (1991) concluded in a study of 14 large multinational companies that:

> We observed that even with the best electronic communication systems, confidence between the team members of a worldwide development project seemed to decay over time. We have sometimes used the expression "the half-life effect of electronic communications" to describe, like the decay of nuclear radiation, this decreasing confidence. Thus, periodic face-to-face contact seems necessary to maintain confidence at a level high enough to promote effective team work. (p. 56)
>
> --A.. DeMeyer

The electronic networks include E-mail, fax machines, and computer networks. List and explain how three specific properties of electronic networks might explain this "half-life effect."

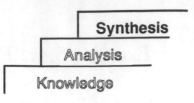
Case 5.1: Diagnosing Channel Capacity Problems

Purpose: Learn how to choose appropriate communication channels.

Situation: Your consulting firm has been hired to examine the effectiveness of a local organization's communication system. They have given you access to the typical kinds of information sent via various channels. Your mission is to determine if they are utilizing these channels effectively.

Method:

1. Select an actual company to evaluate.

2. Gather relevant information about the organization's use of the various channels.

3. Analyze the information gathered in Step 2.

4. Evaluate the general effectiveness of the organization's information system.

5. Make specific recommendations, if necessary.

6. Provide a rationale for Steps 2 through 5.

Case 5.2: Determining Channel Mix and Usage

Purpose: Determine how to select and effectively use different communication channels.

Situation: A paper mill is experiencing "communication problems." Upon investigation you determine that there are three major problems:

• Employees do not feel adequately informed about the direction of the company
• Employees are not adequately informed about day-to-day changes
• There are shift-to-shift and department-to-department communication problems

There are four primary channels:
• Monthly employee newsletter
• Bulletin boards at the time clocks
• Departmental meetings held at the discretion of the manager
• Weekly production reports

Facts about the plant
• 800 employees (150 office staff)
• unionized, with four rotating shifts
• located on a 1/2 mile stretch of a river
• 40 departments
• highly profitable

The company states its values as: customer-focused quality, safety, and empowered employees. The CEO has an MBA from Harvard and an undergraduate degree from MIT. He is an engineer by training but has excellent interpersonal communication skills. He is committed to "Managing By Walking Around." He is well liked by the employees but, in a plant this large, he says: "it's difficult to keep in touch with everyone." In his library-like office he talked about his vision of having a "world-class communication system." How should he spend his limited resources in accomplishing this vision?

Objective:
1. Determine if they need any new channels.
2. Design the proper channel mix for the various communicative functions.
3. Describe how these channels should be utilized. Consider such elements as the content, frequency of their usage, and the audience.
4. Describe how the information should be presented to the CEO.
5. Provide your rationale for Objectives 1 to 4.

Chapter 6: Performance Feedback

Chapter Summary

An effective feedback system seeks to improve employee performance so as to increase organizational performance. However, many employees express low levels of satisfaction with the feedback system in their organization.

A successful feedback system incorporates the following elements:
1. *Employees know their job responsibilities*
2. *Employees know the standards by which they are being evaluated*
3. *There exists an effective informal feedback system*
4. *There exists an effective formal feedback system*

The formal feedback process can be enhanced if the manager follows several guidelines in developing the message:
- *communicate the exact purpose and importance of the interview*
- *be specific and descriptive when making evaluations, rather than evaluative*
- *avoid commenting on personality characteristics*
- *capitalize on employee motivations: link the motivators of employees to critical objectives*

An effective manager realizes that the method is as important as the message. Therefore, the manager needs to consider such things as deciding on a useful evaluation tool (rating scales, ranking methods, critical incidents) to achieve the purpose, using feedback from the task itself, not from the supervisor ("task-inherent" feedback), and using past performance as a bridge to future performance.

Learning Objectives

After studying this chapter, you will be able to:

- discuss some underlying principles of performance feedback

- describe how to implement a successful feedback system

- critique and conduct a performance appraisal interview

Key Terms and Concepts

Chapter Outline

I. Fundamental principles of feedback
   A. Everyone, whether they acknowledge it or not, has standards of performance
   B. The ultimate goal of an effective feedback system is the mutual identification of, performance of, and commitment to the standards
   C. Performance standards are necessary to maintain corporate integrity and develop employee potential
   D. Everyone "receives" feedback about their performance
   E. Few employees receive useful feedback
   F. Both positive and negative deviations from the standards should be noted
   G. Standards of performance should be regularly and systematically re-evaluated

II. Implementing a successful feedback system: Questions to address
   A. Do employees know their job responsibilities?
   B. Do employees know the standards by which they are being evaluated?
   C. Is the informal feedback system effective?
      1. Reasons for problems with informal feedback systems
         a. Many managers don't take the time
         b. Many managers don't notice performance unless there are difficulties
      2. The message: Types of information that can be communicated daily
         a. Agreed-upon standards
         b. Uncommunicated performance standards
         c. Character qualities
      3. The method
         a. Link praise to attributes valued by the company

      b. Link criticism to a larger positive context

      c. Feedback should be maximally informative and minimally evaluative

D. Is the formal feedback system effective?

  1. Reasons for problems with formal feedback systems

      a. Many managers react negatively to the process because it is used to accomplish multiple goals that are often incompatible

      b. Many managers feel compelled to inflate ratings

      c. Many managers resist because they feel like they are "playing God"

  2. The message

      a. Communicate the exact purpose for the interview

      b. Communicate the importance of the interview

      c. Be specific and descriptive when making evaluations

      d. Avoid commenting on personality characteristics

      e. Capitalize on employee motivations

  3. The method

      a. Decide on a useful evaluation tool

      b. Utilize "task-inherent" feedback

      c. Assign employees specific tasks to prepare for the interview

      d. Consider how the appraisal process is influenced by interpersonal needs

      e. Use past performance as a bridge to the future

Exercise 6.1: Evaluating Statements About Performance Feedback

Synthesis

Analysis

Knowledge

Based on the discussion in Chapter 6 note which of the following statements are true (T) and which are false (F).

1. Many managers resist performance appraisal because they feel like they are "playing God."

2. Most feedback systems have only one objective.

3. It is appropriate for a manager to focus on an employee's personality during a performance appraisal.

4. Most employees do not want to know how they are performing.

5. If a manager does an effective job of providing feedback on a day-to-day basis, there is little need to perform a regular performance appraisal.

6. Management by objectives is a process in which the supervisor sets the goals for the employee and the employee determines how the goals will be achieved.

7. Basically there are only two methods to measure performance: (a) essay approach, and (b) rating scales.

8. Many managers feel compelled by the system to inflate their ratings.

9. Praise tends to be a stronger motivator than criticism.

10. Task-inherent feedback is an effective replacement for the formal appraisal process.

11. The manager should use past performance as a bridge to future achievement.

12. As long as the manager is straightforward during the appraisal interview, there are few motivations for the employee to distort the manager's assessment.

Exercise 6.2: Identifying Specific Feedback Problems

There are four fundamental issues in resolving performance feedback problems:

- Do employees know their job responsibilities? (JR)
- Do employees know the standards of evaluation? (S)
- Is the informal feedback system effective? (IF)
- Is the formal feedback system effective? (FF)

Using the abbreviations above, determine the appropriate category for the following comments from employees. Then suggest a potential remedy.

1. "I have no control over 50% of the items on the performance appraisal form."

2. "The only time I ever hear from my boss is when I 'screw up."

3. "I've got so many responsibilities. No one gives me guidelines about what is most important."

4. "Look, I know my job, but I don't have a clue as to how I'm evaluated."

5. "Last year my boss gave me a form and I just signed it. About 2 weeks later I found out that was my performance appraisal."

6. "I'm completely bewildered about how my manager comes up with the numbers for rating me."

7. "I just wish some day someone would give me a pat on the back."

Exercise 6.3: Praising Employees

Synthesis

Analysis

Knowledge

For each situation below, suggest an appropriate message of praise for the employee. Recall that in Chapter 6 it was suggested that both the specific behavior and character quality are praised.

1. An employee of a savings and loan puts in many overtime hours to complete a project on time for a client.

2. An employee discovers a brand new way to process bills that saves the company thousands of dollars.

3. A manager smoothly implements a change to an advanced computer system in her department. She does this despite numerous "bugs" in the new system and anticipated personnel objections.

Exercise 6.4: Criticizing Employees

Critique the managerial choices in the following situations. Be sure to examine both the positive and negative aspects of the decisions.

1. An enthusiastic employee embarked on a new promotional project. He had put a great deal of work into the project, including a number of extra hours. However, the results proved ambiguous at best and senior management viewed the project as a failure. In the past, the employee had a number of excellent ideas. The employee was well aware of the "less-than-spectacular results." In this case, his manager decided to say nothing about the project and results.

2. A grocery store clerk came to work about 7 minutes late twice in the past 2 weeks. The employee is a solid performer and has worked at the job a couple of years. The manager chose not to confront the employee the first two times because it had not been a problem before. She made this choice knowing that the employee's tardiness inconvenienced other clerks. The third time the employee came in 10 minutes late, the manager said:

   "What's going on? This is the third time this month you've been late. I can't tolerate this any more. You are inconsiderate of your fellow employees and the customers. Now, what are we going to do to solve this problem?"

3. A new supervisor attended her first meeting with fellow supervisors. Her enthusiasm was obvious and she had a number of useful suggestions to improve office productivity. When other supervisors made suggestions she listened and on a few occasions she said, "Well, I don't think that will work for the following reasons." Then she would list the reasons. Her comments were generally quite perceptive. However, a few of the other supervisors were offended. The supervisor's manager called her into the office the next day. The manager discussed a number of matters and concluded the conversation in the following manner:

"You made a number of good points during the meeting yesterday, but a few of the other supervisors didn't care for the spirit of your comments. I think we need your new ideas but I thought you ought to know how some of the others feel."

Exercise 6.5: Thought Quote

In an insightful article, Michael Beer commented about the dilemmas of the feedback process. After reading his comments below, suggest three specific ways to address his concerns.

> The core of the problem is that supervisor's organizational roles as judge can lead them into communicating and defending their evaluation to subordinates at the very time they are trying to develop an open two-way dialogue for a valid information exchange and development. The defensiveness that results may take the form of open hostility and denials, but it may also take the form of passivity and "surface compliance". In either case, the subordinate doesn't really accept or understand the feedback. Thus, those subordinates who may need development the most may learn the least. (p. 20)
>
> -- M. Beer

Case 6.1: Appraising the Appraisal Interview

Purpose: To learn how to conduct an appraisal interview effectively from the interviewer's and interviewee's perspective.

Situation: You are coaching a manager and employee on how to improve the appraisal interview process. You observe the following interview.

MANAGER: Welcome Pat. I'm sorry we've delayed this meeting so many times. It has been tough coordinating our schedules.

EMPLOYEE: That's OK, I've been rather anxious about this. You know this is my first appraisal since I started a year ago.

MANAGER: I've tried to keep you informed along the way.

EMPLOYEE: But you've been very busy.

MANAGER: We all are. But dealing with pressure is part of the business.

EMPLOYEE: Of course.

MANAGER: Maybe we should begin. I want to start by reviewing your job responsibilities, then I want to go into the areas of strength and conclude with areas of improvement. If you have any questions along the way, just fire away.

EMPLOYEE: I'm ready.

MANAGER: As you know, a year ago we established the position of communications coordinator. So we are still defining the precise responsibilities of the job. We primarily envisioned the job involving four principle areas: (1) editing the employee newsletter, (2) supervising the bulletin boards (3) advising management on communication strategies, and (4) producing the in-house video magazine.

EMPLOYEE: Between myself and a staff of three employees, we are trying to cover those areas. I think we have formed a pretty strong team over the course of the year.

MANAGER: That's true, but I've got to look at the department's productivity in terms of organizational goals.

EMPLOYEE: As a staff, we understand that.

MANAGER: In terms of strengths, I want to compliment you on coordinating the various communication activities around the organization. Our idea about pulling all the communication tasks together in one department seems to have worked out. You've done a great job coordinating those efforts. As a result, we've eliminated unnecessary duplication of efforts and increased the productivity of our staff.

EMPLOYEE: We've been able to target our communication vehicles more precisely in order to serve the various audiences in the company. That was one of our first tasks.

MANAGER: Well you did a good job in that area. You also have done a nice job revising the newsletter. It looks more professional than in the past. Readership is up and the employees that I've talked to have commented favorably. I think your work on this demonstrates a flair of creativity that should be useful in other tasks.

EMPLOYEE: I made the newsletter our first priority because I knew it was an important piece in our communication program.

MANAGER: There a couple of areas I'd like to see improve over the next year. First, I've been disappointed in the quarterly video magazine. What are your goals?

EMPLOYEE: To be honest with you, I haven't really focused on it. We have been consumed with getting the newsletter on track.

MANAGER: As a supervisor you've got to be able to direct several projects simultaneously. Frankly, I'm embarrassed by the quality--fortunately very few employees watch it. How do you see the video magazine improving productivity around here?

EMPLOYEE: I have one employee who has sole responsibility for the video magazine. I'll have to get him going on it.

MANAGER: Look, what I'm talking about is the strategic purpose. One of the key points of our Total Quality program is improving communication by cutting down the lag time in the feedback cycle. What I want to know is how does this activity help us do that?

EMPLOYEE: When we set our department goals next week, I'll be sure to get on this guy, so that we can answer those questions.

MANAGER: But strategic issues should be your concern--it's hard for this guy to produce a quality product if he doesn't know what the goals are.

EMPLOYEE: I'll sit down and talk to him next week. You said we did a good job on the newsletter, right?

MANAGER: Right.

EMPLOYEE: Then give us some time and we'll do a good job on the video. I promise you that.

MANAGER: OK, let me just briefly mention my other concern. I'm concerned that you haven't developed a plan for how your department fits into the broader organizational goals based on TQM (Total Quality Management).

EMPLOYEE: But you said we put together a quality newsletter.

MANAGER: True, but what I'm talking about is a more strategic focus, rather than one on departmental activities. I want to know how all the communication activities in the business are working together to meet our strategic objectives. That was the main rationale for creating this department.

EMPLOYEE: By sitting in on the strategic planning sessions, I know what our strategic vision is.

MANAGER: But I don't think you know how to think strategically. I'm talking about the big picture. I want to know how the department is LINKED INTO the corporation's goals. I don't see it. I don't hear you talking about it in this discussion. I mean even though the newsletter has "improved," it is important to ask questions about how it fits into the overall strategic mission of the company. For example, what is the rationale behind the article selection? How do the articles relate to corporate objectives? These are the kinds of issues I want you to grapple with.

EMPLOYEE: How am I supposed to think strategically when I've got to put out a newsletter every 2 weeks, a video magazine every quarter, sit in on countless meetings, and advise speaker's on their presentations?

MANAGER: You have a staff.

EMPLOYEE: Don't you think that my staff is a cohesive team?

MANAGER: Of course, but that's not the point.

EMPLOYEE: The point is my team needs more time to solve some of these problems. After all, we've only been together for a year. You don't expect a losing football team to win the Super Bowl after a year under a new head coach.

MANAGER: You've got a point, but I'm just trying to provide you some guidance.

EMPLOYEE: We appreciate that, but you have to admit we have put together a pretty good team.

MANAGER: I see that.

EMPLOYEE: Give us a little more time and we will iron out all these difficulties.

MANAGER: Agreed, but at least you know my concerns. There are the positives of the newsletter and the elimination of duplication.

EMPLOYEE: So basically I'm doing a great job and we just need some time to work out our mission.

MANAGER: I'd agree with that assessment as long as you understand where the problems are.

EMPLOYEE: I do and I'm glad we had a chance to chat about my team. I'll be sure to tell them how well they are doing.

MANAGER: I need you to sign this form on the bottom.

Based on your observations, address the following questions in providing feedback to the manager and employee.

1. What are the motivations of the employee? manager?

2. How well does the manager tap into the employee's motivations and vice versa?

3. What do you think will happen to the employee's performance over the next year?

4. How effective was the interview? Why?

5. What could the manager do to improve the effectiveness of the interview? The employee?

Method:

1 Justify your responses to the questions above.

2. Provide the strategic and tactical rationale for how you are going to provide feedback to the manager and employee.

Case 6.2: Managing the "One Minute Manager"

Purpose: To create a strategic rationale for a performance feedback system.

Situation:
Your boss is the manager of the personnel department. Your department has been assigned to develop a new performance appraisal system for the company. The system in place now has fallen into disrepute through lack of use. Your boss is always open to new ideas and has just read *The One Minute Manager* by Blanchard and Johnson. She thinks this book is the answer to her prayers. She wants to use this book as the training tool and conceptual framework for the new performance appraisal system. She has asked you to provide a critique of the book and develop a 2-hour training program about the philosophy behind appraising employee using the book as a stepping stone. She has asked you to meet with her next week and outline the entire content of the session complete with exercises, readings, and handouts. She is particularly concerned that you do a good job "selling" the process.

Method:

1. Prepare a critique of the book.

2. Develop an outline of a training program with objectives, content, and exercises.

3. Provide the rationale for your decisions.

4. Discuss how you will present your ideas to the boss and the rationale for your approach.

Chapter 7: Communicating Change

Chapter Summary

Managing and communicating change may be the greatest challenge facing today's managers. Events such as personnel developments, reorganizations, sudden impacts of a political crisis, or shifts in consumer preferences can force radical changes on the organization.

Organizations have different orientations toward change that define who can suggest, institute, and act on a new idea. A "management orientation" is indicative of an organization where top management dictates that the change be carried out through the chain of command. In contrast, the "employee orientation" defines an organization where ideas for changes and methods of implementation are encouraged from employees. The "integrative approach" suggests that the orientation that is most effective depends on the situation. A successful organization uses a strategy where the natural strengths of each approach are realized.

Changes can be characterized on a continuum from routine to nonroutine. Communicating nonroutine changes, like incorporating new technology in the workplace, is a more difficult challenge. When employees are faced with major changes, many will pass through stages of reaction similar to experiencing a death: denial and isolation, anger, bargaining, depression, and acceptance. A skillful manager can ease the transition by being sensitive to these stages of reaction. There are actions that identify each reaction stage and appropriate actions that the manager can take.

There are nine principles that are suggested to ensure that the change is communicated most effectively. For example, it is important to choose the appropriate communication channel. The more nonroutine the change, the more important it is to use a dynamic channel. In addition it is critical to anticipate possible resistance points, such as fear of economic loss, anxiety over the unknown, and social disruptions. The effective manager anticipates these issues and develops appropriate responses.

Learning Objectives

After studying this chapter, you will be able to:

- describe and identify three orientations to change

- discuss several misconceptions of organizational change

- identify different types of organizational changes and stages in coping with nonroutine changes

- analyze how to strategically communicate change and develop a communication change program

Key Terms and Concepts

orientations to change   pp. 175-178
management orientation   p. 175
employee orientation   p. 176
intrapreneurship   p. 176
integrative approach   pp. 177-178
routine change   p. 183
nonroutine change   p. 185
psychological stages in coping with death/change   pp. 185-189
communicating change at reaction stages   p. 190
unifying vision   p.194
channel selection based on degree of change   p. 197
probability of resistance to change based on degree of change   p. 198
resistance points and organizational developmental stage   p. 199

Chapter Outline

I. Approaches to change
    A. Management orientation
    B. Employee orientation
    C. Integrative approach

II. Misconceptions of organizational change
    A. Change is unnatural
    B. Change is always disruptive
    C. Change is always progressive
    D. Change is always stressful
    E. Change indicates that previous practices were incorrect
    F. Real change is only born out of a crisis

III. A continuum of organizational changes
   A. Routine changes
   B. Nonroutine changes: stages in coping with grief and/or change
      1. Denial and isolation
      2. Anger
      3. Bargaining
      4. Depression
      5. Acceptance

IV. How to communicate change strategically
   A. Determine how the organization has communicated past changes
   B. Know what needs to be changed
   C. Recognize that the meaning of the change is more important than the change itself
   D. Develop a unifying vision of the change that energizes and motivates employees
   E. Recognize that change cannot be perfectly planned
   F. Provide as much information to employees as is reasonably possible
   G. Choose appropriate communication channels
   H. Anticipate possible resistance points
   I. Consider the timing of the messages

Exercise 7.1: Identifying Approaches to Change

For each of the following statements, determine the implicit orientation to change. Use the following abbreviations to make your choices: Management orientation (M), Employee orientation (E), or Integrative orientation (I). Provide your rationale below each statement.

<u>Statement</u>	<u>Orientation</u>

a. This approach encourages employees to have input into changes and methods of implementation.

b. The main assumption of this approach is that those in leadership positions are in a better position to recognize the need for change.

c. The heart of this approach is intrapreneurship.

d. The central focus of this approach is not on who champions the change but on what is right in the given situation.

e. This approach may result in a stifling of the innovative spirit of the employees.

Exercise 7.2:   Identifying Stages of Change

The following actions are characteristics of various stages employees may pass through in dealing with an organizational change.   Identify the stage: Denial (D), Anger (A), Bargaining (B), Depression (DP), or Acceptance (AC).

Identifying actions	Stage
a. trying to make deals	_____
b. resuming a sense of "normalcy"	_____
c. being confrontive	_____
d. not showing up for meetings	_____
e. contemplating sabotage	_____
f. appearing listless	_____
g. appearing short fused	_____
h. being untalkative and apathetic	_____

Exercise 7.3: Selecting Communicative Strategies for Different Degrees of Change

Synthesis

Analysis

Knowledge

Communicative strategies differ depending on the degree of change. Fill in the chart below to indicate how important each factor is in the various change situations. Use the following designations: H = High, M = Medium, L = Low.

	Routine Change	Moderate Change	Large-Scale Change
a. Need for a dynamic channel			
b. Need to discourage receiver from asking a lot of questions			
c. Need for persuasive appeals			
d. Need for highly credible channels			
e. Need to economize language through jargon			
f. Need to reduce the number of channels used to communicate			
g. Need to standardize information display			
h. Need to "contextualize" information in terms of organizational vision			

How likely are the following to occur in the various change situations? Respond with an H, M, or L.

i. Probability of resistance			
j. Probability of rumors			
k. Likelihood sender will know receiver's information needs			
l. Likelihood that interpersonal relationships will become a resistance point			

65

Exercise 7.4: Analyzing Interaction Effects

Many of the issues in the previous exercise are related. For example, the need for dynamic channels (issue a) is linked to the probability of rumors (issue j). Dynamic channels help reduce rumors because they can more effectively address founded or unfounded concerns of employees. When the probability of rumors is less, the need for dynamic channels is reduced. Listed below are some other key relationships. Explain the nature of the relationship.

1. The likelihood the sender will know the receiver's information needs and the need to reduce the number of channels used to communicate.

2. The need to standardize information display and the probability of resistance.

3. The probability of resistance and the need to discourage the receiver from asking a lot of questions.

4. The need to economize language through jargon and the need for a dynamic channel.

5. The need to "contextualize" information and the need for persuasive appeals.

Exercise 7.5: Thought Quote

In the following quotation, Jack Welch, the CEO of General Electric, makes a bold statement about change. If he is correct, then when are the implications for how change needs to be communicated?   Do you agree with his statement?

> When I try to summarize what I've learned since 1981, one of the big lessons is that change has no constituency. People like the status quo. They like the way it was. When you start changing things, the good old days look better and better. You've got to be prepared for massive resistance. Incremental change doesn't work very well in the type of transformation GE has gone through. If your change isn't big enough, the bureaucracy can beat you. When you get leaders who confuse popularity with leadership, who just nibble away at things, nothing changes. (p. 88)
>
> -- Jack Welch

Case 7.1: Implementing a Change

Purpose: To learn how to communicate change effectively in an organization.

Situation:

1. You are advising the CEO and founder of a 150-person telemarketing firm. The major divisions of the company are: Marketing, Telemarketing, Distribution, Computer Staff, and Administration.

   The company has been quite successful in marketing nuts, bolts and other hardware to manufacturers across the nation. The company continues to grow since its founding 12 years ago. The CEO credits the company's "customer focus" as the major reason for sustained growth.

2. The CEO believes that the company's next growth spurt will be the result of the "wave of the future" involving computer technology. Accordingly, the firm is set to test market the "Scanner Technology," which is a device that acts much like the scanner at grocery stores in which items pass over computerized bar codes.

3. The firm would like to use this technology with major accounts that purchase many of the firm's products. The scanner saves both the firm and the customer a tremendous amount of time. In addition, accuracy is increased because the orders are no longer taken over the phone and recorded by hand.

4. The technology involves giving the client the scanner to pass over bar-coded bins in their warehouse and transmitting the data directly to your company's computers.

5. The CEO is personally committed to a lifetime employment policy. He is well regarded by employees and is known to be a "gifted communicator" who is always coming up with new ideas. Once he is sure that the idea will work, he moves forward quickly with aggressive and detailed timetables.

6. The last time the firm instituted a major change, there was an increase in personnel through a redistribution of employees. Yet, despite the CEO's best efforts to communicate effectively, many employees were quite anxious and rumors ran rampant through the organization.

7. In general, the change will have the most impact on the Telemarketing department, which is 50% of the work force. Instead of selling and taking orders, these employees will be more involved in customer service such as dealing with complaints.

8. At this point, the vice presidents are aware of the change and are quite excited about it. Employees in the computer department have already begun to develop the appropriate software. Other employees have only heard about the program through the grapevine. The CEO wants to avoid the mistakes of his last effort.

9. At this stage the firm is testing out the concept with only five clients. The company plans to proceed as follows:
   a. Test in five large markets.
   b. Revise, based on feedback.
   c. Market in other large markets.

10. As the consultant, your objective is to advise the CEO on how to proceed at this point.

Objectives:

1. Using the information above, decide how and when you would go about informing employees of the changes. Also, specify what information they should receive.

2. Determine what channels of communication you would use.

3. Determine how you would present your plan to the CEO.

4. Most importantly, provide the rationale for all of your choices.

Case 7.2: Communicating Routine Changes

Purpose: To develop a set of principles for communicating routine changes.

Method:

1. Go to several local organizations and collect 10 to 15 examples ("artifacts") of how they communicate routine changes.

2. Determine the level of effectiveness for each communication artifact from the perspective of the intended audience. (You could use interviews or short surveys.)

3. Analyze each communication artifact. For example, look at language, channel, graphic, timing, and contextual choices. (You might find it helpful to look at Chapters 4 and 5 again.)

4. Measure the overall effectiveness of the "artifacts" based on your findings in Steps 2 and 3.

Objectives:

1. Rank order all the communication artifacts from best to worst. (If you prefer you could use three categories: Best, Average, and Poor.)

2. Explain your rationale for the ranking.

3. Develop a list of "10 key principles for communicating routine changes" that you could use in any organization.

4. Provide your rationale, using your research and principles discussed in the book.

Chapter 8: Interdepartmental Communication

Chapter Summary

Departments, by their very nature, perform distinct functions, are physically separated, and have different priorities. They are separated financially by accounting budgets and often speak a different language. In short, departments create barriers. While communication between departments is problematic in most companies, it is an essential source of productivity.

The challenge is how to most effectively manage interdepartmental communication problems. A manager must balance the needs of the "providers" of communication with the needs of the "consumers" of communication. The ideal system would block all redundant information but allow every unique or special inquiry. There are a number of "minor effort" projects, such as job switching and coauthoring of articles that attempt to ease interdepartmental communication problems. In addition, there are approaches such as job rotation, redesigning accounting procedures, and changing office design which are more major efforts that attempt to make interdepartmental communication more effective.

Learning Objectives

After studying this chapter, you will be able to:
- describe the nature and potential problems of departmentalization

- isolate the possible "tension points" departments might face with one another

- identify factors contributing to the barriers between departments

- determine and develop programs companies can implement to effectively manage interdepartmental communication problems

Key Terms and Concepts

departmentalization   p. 206
addition/multiplication factor   p. 214
effect of location on communication   p. 217
job switching   p. 219
job rotation   p. 224
core competency   p. 224

Chapter Outline

I. The nature of departmentalization: generally, departments
   A. perform separate functions
   B. are physically separated
   C. are separated through accounting procedures
   D. separate employees through the authority structure

II. The problems of departmentalization
   A. Poor performance
   B. Unnecessary conflict
   C. Lack of innovation
   D. Overlapping responsibilities
   E. Wasted time
   F. Potential safety hazards

III. Factors contributing to the barriers between departments
   A. Language differences
   B. Priority differences
   C. Rewards and punishments
   D. Category dissimilarities
   E. Rigid procedures
   F. Multiplicative increase of communication linkages with arithmetical increase in departments
   G. Office design

IV. What to do? How to effectively manage interdepartmental communication problems
   A. Minor effort projects
      1. Job switching
      2. Company-wide seminars
      3. Coauthored articles
      4. New product presentations
      5. Brainstorming sessions
      6. Travel
      7. Company-wide gatherings
      8. Office "show and tell"

B. Major effort projects
    1. Job rotation
    2. Redesign of accounting procedures
    3. Change office design
    4. Develop communication policy
    5. Change job descriptions
    6. Change organizational structure

Exercise 8.1: Communication Links

Synthesis

Analysis

Knowledge

Determine the number of communication links as the number of departments in an organization increase.

Ex: A company has three departments. If the company adds a fourth department, how many additional communication links will there be?

Answer: There will be three additional communication links. There are 3 with 3 departments, 6 with 4 departments.

a. A company has seven departments. There are __communication links. If the company adds an eighth department, there will be __ links.

b. There are nine people in a department. There are __ communication links. If there is an additional person added to the department, there will be ____ new communication links.

Exercise 8.2: Techniques to Improve Interdepartmental Communication

Identify the approach that is described.

a. ____ is a major organizational effort in which an employee becomes familiar with another department's jobs and responsibilities and actually performs them over long periods of time. In this type of program, a lateral move is not seen in a negative light but rather as an opportunity to learn more about the complexities of the company.

b. In contrast to "a" above, ____ involves employees from various departments changing jobs for several days to get a feel for the other person's job. Hyatt Hotels is just one example of a corporation that has successfully used this technique to foster more effective communication between departments and to provide insight into how to serve their customers more effectively.

c. Organizations can set up ____ for departments where they meet and share their unique problems. Typically there is no formal agenda and they freely share ideas they freely share ideas without being judged by others.

Exercise 8.3: Identifying Managerial Tendencies

Which of the following interdepartmental issues would most likely surface in organizations dominated by managers with an Arrow (A), Circuit (C), or Dance (D) orientation? Provide your rationale.

_____ a. information overload

_____ b. information underload

_____ c. slow response to interdepartmental requests

_____ d. tendency to adhere to administrative procedures

_____ e. tendency to seek coordination between departments

_____ f. clear organization of tasks by administrative units

_____ g. focus on functional organizational units rather than processes

_____ h. tendency to have problems coordinating communication between the organization's committees

_____ i. tendency for each department to clearly "own" certain geographical spaces in the organization

_____ j. strategically located conference rooms that are "between" the geographical domain of different departments

_____ k. use of face-to-face meetings to resolve most interdepartmental problems

_____ l. use of memos or E-mail to resolve most interdepartmental problems

_____ m. heavy use of unifying themes or values to avoid interdepartmental problems

Exercise 8.4: Thought Quote

In the following quote, the authors of a provocatively titled book, *Improving Performance: How to Manage the White Space on the Organizational Chart,* make an intriguing statement about how to increase organizational productivity. What "opportunities" do you think the authors are describing? What examples come to mind?

> The greatest opportunities for performance improvement often lie in the functional interfaces --those points at which the baton (for example, "production specs") is being passed from one department to another. (p. 69)
>
> --G. Rummler and A. Brache

Case 8.1: Resolving Interdepartmental Communication Issues

Purpose: To understand how to resolve interdepartmental communication problems.

Situation: You are the new president of an HMO and you have detected some "grave" interdepartmental communication problems. Listed below are some relevant facts:

1. In 1984 the company had 6 employees; today there are 187.

2. The departments that are having the problems are Member Services and Medical Services.

3. Member Services employees directly interface with the public and answer their questions regarding benefits, accessing health care, and resolving claim problems. The 10 workers in this department tend to have public relations or human relations backgrounds. They are "relations-oriented" kinds of people.

4. Medical Services employees have contact with providers of services (hospitals, physicians), the Member Services department, and, on rare occasion, clients. The 24 workers have medical backgrounds such as a nursing degree. Their duties include triaging, and reviewing all emergency room claims or questionable claims. In short, they provide specific medical interpretations of the benefits outlined in the contract.

5. Each department is under separate lines of authority and the departments are physically separated by a long corridor.

6. Interaction between the two departments is usually initiated by a Member Services representative who is inquiring about a claim for a client. The inquiries typically center around triage, delayed payments due to investigation by Medical Services, or interpretations regarding specific medical treatments.

7. The following is a list of problems uncovered so far:

- An employee in Member Services remarked: "Can you tell me who does what over there? I call four different people to get one answer and all I hear is 'so and so' is doing that job today. 'So and so' says the next person is doing it. Often we are shuffled full circle back to the original person with no answer."(See sample page from the company telephone book)

- A report on the telephone usage of the Member Services department indicated that telephone efficiency was down. (This was computed by analyzing the number of calls and the length of time a client waited to speak to an employee.)

- The supervisor of the Medical Services department indicated that her department was receiving numerous calls for different Member Services asking for the same information.

- Member Services representatives typically are unfamiliar with some of the medical terminology, particularly new treatments, that are used by Medical Services.

Method:

1. Specify the precise action you would take if you were the president of this HMO.

2. Specify the approach you would use in presenting the proposal to the departments.

3. Provide the rationale for the approach and proposal.

Telephone Directory
(Sample Page)

Conference Rooms
Boardroom 623
Claims 869
Marketing 545
Medical Mgr. 609
Receptionist 896

Coord. of Benefits 827
Sheryl C. 551
Laury L. 824
Louis J. 831
Denis J. 600 Supr.

Denial
Kathy R. 840

Finance
Bill F. 817 Ofcr.
Tom M. 845 Supr.
Glenn R. 808 Mgr.
Bev R. 837
Sandy S. 836

Finance/Medical Analysis
Bob A. 807 Mgr.
Susan C. 699
Rita D. 829 Supr.
Ginnie P. 844

Health Services
Susan 815 Ofcr.
Cindy C. 883 Sec.
Brenda D. 812

Dr. Dave 625

Ellen C. 660

Mailroom
Gloria - Page
Pat E. 884

Ginny C. 338
Laurey B. 823
Phil C. 880 Supr.
Traci B. 683
Cindy C. 624 Supr.

Medical Services 806
Jean B. 814 Supr.
Lisa G. 678
Judy C. 622
Jenny D. 813 Mgr.
Audrey 637
Jodie C. 515 Sec.
Shari A. 816
Marlene 620 Supr.

Member Services 802
Katy B. 891
Gail C. 897
Karen F. 616 Supr.
Joan H. 855 Supr.
Renee H. 617
Cindy V. 839

Triage Services
Kim A. 2nd Shift
Sue H. 2nd Shift
Jodie S. 3rd Shift
Wendy S. 3rd Shift
Bonnie 628 Supr.

Sue A. 698

Underwriting
Clara S. 602 Supr.
Karen M. 606

Provider Relations
Ann A. 640
Darrin E. 864
Jill H. 645
Sharon K. 809 Supr.
Julie S. 613
Shawn S. 890 Sec.
Linda S. 641

Misc.
Duplicating 887
Fax # 471-0000
Kitchen 670

CRC 841
Karen K. 849
Jayne S. 603

Executive Offices
Phil C. 222 CEO
Laurey B. 111 CFO

Case 8.2: Stapling Yourself to an Order

Purpose: To understand the nuances of how information is filtered by different departments

Situation: You have been asked to "staple yourself to a customer's order" by the president of the company. Her objective is to get a handle on the bottlenecks and different perceptions of an order as it passes through the various departments. She is particularly interested in:

1. How long does it take to process an order at each stage?
2. How do different departments prioritize orders? What criteria are used?
3. What information is unclear or missing on the order?
4. How does each department handle problems with an order?
5. Do different departments have a sense of the "whole system"?
6. How does each department filter the information?
7. What view of the "customer" does each department have?

The president has asked you to do this because, she is committed to "customer-focused quality" and she wonders if the order management cycle (OMC) is effectively serving customer needs. She gave you a copy of an article in *Harvard Business Review* by Shapiro, Rangan, and Sviokla (July-August 1992) titled, "Staple Yourself to an Order." She underlined the following paragraph:

> In the course of the order management cycle, every time the order is handled, the customer is handled. Every time the order sits unattended, the customer sits unattended. Paradoxically, the best way to be customer-oriented is to go beyond customers and products to the order; the moment of truth occurs at every step of the OMC, and every employee in the company who affects the OMC is the equivalent of a front-line worker. Ultimately, it is the order that connects the customer to the company in a systematic and company-wide fashion. (pp. 113-114)

Based on your data gathering, she would like you to make recommendations on the following issues.

1. How effective is the OMC?
2. What are the key strengths (weaknesses) of the system?
3. How can customer service be improved?

Method:

1. Select an order cycle to explore. There are a variety of different types of OMCs your could explore, including: a purchase order at a small local factory, opening a new account at a bank, or registration procedures at a college. Try to pick a cycle that is not too complicated; even reconciling the perspectives of three or four departments is difficult.

2. Describe the cycle in detail.

3. Evaluate the cycle using the president's questions.

4. Provide recommendations based on your evaluation.

Chapter 9: Communicating the Innovative Spirit

Chapter Summary

The organizations that will survive in the future will be those that are innovative. This chapter discusses the process of innovation and suggests ways in which the organization can foster the innovative spirit.

The process of innovation is one of "winnowing down" the possibilities to select several that can be useful to the organization. The process begins with "idea generation," where the emphasis is on generating a multitude of novel ideas in a nonevaluative setting. The process continues with "feasibility analysis" which, through experiments or test runs, addresses the possibility of the ideas. "Reality testing" addresses how practical the ideas are. Do they provide a reasonable return? Do they fit with organizational objectives? Finally, those that survive may pass to the "implementation stage," where the idea is acted on. Organizational barriers, such as too many rules and regulations, lack of corporate resources, lack of commitment to research, and a short-term focus, can occur at any point during this process and hinder its progress.

To develop an environment that fosters innovation, the organization needs to design a system that encourages the flow of innovative ideas and increases the probability that useful ideas are provided speedy passage through the process. The chapter discusses 10 guidelines that will accomplish this, such as requiring innovation as part of the job, developing company programs that encourage innovation, and eliminating lengthy proposal procedures.

Learning Objectives

After studying this chapter, you will be able to:

- describe some misconceptions of innovation

- identify the phases of the innovation process

- identify evaluation criteria, critical questions, and organizational barriers representative of each phase of the process

- identify activities that commonly occur at each stage in the process

- describe the four possible outcomes of an innovation

- develop guidelines for establishing a system that encourages innovation

- develop a list of "what not to do"/ elements that discourage innovation

- critique a novel idea while not discouraging an employee's innovative spirit

- devise a list of channels of communication that are most compatible with each stage of the innovation process

Key Terms and Concepts

Chapter Outline

I. Misconceptions of innovation
    A. Innovation is risky
    B. Innovation is always the product of the revolutionary "big" idea or grand scheme
    C. Innovation is solely the product of a few great minds
    D. Innovation is product-focused
    E. Creativity is the same as innovation

II. The phases of the innovation process
    A. Idea generation
    B. Feasibility analysis

C. Reality testing
D. Implementation
E. Implications of this process
  1. There are different evaluation criteria at the various stages of the innovative process
  2. Organizational barriers can occur at any point in the innovative process
  3. The time line for the innovative process is elastic
  4. An overemphasis on any one stage can become problematic

III. Measuring success and failure: four possible outcomes of an innovation
  A. Potential success
  B. Enduring success
  C. Temporary success
  D. Failure
  E. Implications
    1. Results do not determine if a new idea is a success or, failure
    2. Present success is no guarantee of future success
    3. The actual innovation is only the tip of the iceberg

IV. "Stop and Go Signs": Guidelines for establishing a system that encourages innovation
  A. Develop a formal corporate policy on innovation
  B. Require innovation
  C. Develop company programs that encourage innovation
  D. Make every employee an innovator
  E. Allow "secret" persistence
  F. Eliminate lengthy proposal procedures
  G. Foster informal communication
  H. Reward innovation
  I. Learn how to reject novel ideas properly
  J. Educate employees about the innovative process

V. "Blue Ribbons and Red Tape": Winston Churchill's invention of the tank
  A. There is a speculative nature to any innovation
  B. Churchill was the First Lord of the Admiralty when he proposed and financed the tank
  C. The saga of the tank demonstrates the need for someone being the "champion of the idea"

Exercise 9.1: Describing the Innovation Process

Fill in the missing blanks.

STAGE	EVALUATION CRITERIA	CRITICAL QUESTIONS
Idea generation		
	possibility	
Reality testing		Does the idea fit with organizational objectives?
	activity	

Exercise 9.2: Identifying Activities in the Innovation Process

Match the following activities to the appropriate stage in the innovation process:

Activities	Stage
_____ 1. Conducting experiments and test runs	a. Idea generation
_____ 2. Assigning responsibilities for action phase	b. Feasibility analysis
_____ 3. Brainstorming	c. Reality testing
_____ 4. Profitability analysis	d. Implementation
_____ 5. Creativity emphasized	
_____ 6. Allocating funds for final project	
_____ 7. Computer simulations	

Exercise 9.3: Barriers to Innovation

Match each of the following "barriers" to the stage in the innovation process where the resistance is most likely faced.

Barriers	Stage
_____ 1. Highly structured organizational climate	a. Idea generation
_____ 2. Nobody has responsibility for the implementation	b. Feasibility analysis
	c. Reality testing
_____ 3. Inadequate research on the potential return or marketability of the idea	d. Implementation
_____ 4. Lack of corporate resources to dedicate to research	
_____ 5. Too many rules and regulations	

Exercise 9.4: Determining Channel Usage

A variety of channels are listed below. Place a check mark by those channels that appear compatible with each stage of the innovation process. (Note: the channels may be compatible with more than one stage.)

	Idea Generation	Feasibility Analysis	Reality Testing	Implementation
Face-to-Face				
Telephone				
Formal Presentation				
Memos				
Fax				
E-mail				
Computer Conference				
Bulletin Board				
Voice Mail				
Teleconference				
Group Meeting				
Video Conference				

Exercise 9.5: Channel Summary

Summarize your findings from Exercise 9.4 by noting the channels that are most compatible with each stage in the innovation process. Provide the rationale for your choices.

Idea Generation

Channels   Rationale
-
-
-
-
-

Feasibility Analysis

Channels   Rationale
-
-
-
-
-

Reality Testing

Channels   Rationale
-
-
-
-
-

Implementation

Channels   Rationale
-
-
-
-
-

Exercise 9.6: Hindering the Innovative Spirit

David Letterman is famous for his "Top 10" lists. Based on your readings, develop your own "Top 10" list of ways to squash the innovative spirit of employees.

1. example: Demand perfection

2.

3.

4.

5.

6.

7.

8.

9.

10.

Exercise 9.7: Thought Quote

In Henry Petroski's intriguing book, *The Pencil: A History of Design and Circumstance*, he makes the statement about the nature of innovation. What are the implications of his ideas for a manager trying to foster innovation? Try to describe three actions implied by Petroski's notions and three actions managers should avoid.

> The origins of pencils, bridges, and other artifacts of craftsmanship and early engineering can be imagined to belong almost more to mythology than to history, for it is the nature of much tinkering, inventing, and even engineering to save little of what is superseded. Ideas that are improved upon are displaced in much the same way the old files on computer disks are written over with the new, and the artifacts that are improved upon are often discarded or cannibalized for a new improved product. What remains of original thoughts or things will be as obliterated as the first pencil marks on a much-used palimpsest. (p. 94)
>
> --H. Petroski

Case 9.1: Implementing an Employee Innovation Program

Purpose: To develop an effective program to encourage employee innovation.

Situation: You've been asked to advise a manager in a local manufacturing plant about how to implement an employee suggestion system. The manager is under "orders" to develop this system because the president has just toured another plant that has an "effective" suggestion system.

The manager provides the following background:

We've tried this twice before and it never really worked. The first program started about 5 years ago and was called the Performance Improvement Program or PIP. Employees were informed about the program and were shown how to fill out the necessary form. These were the main problems:

1. Many people came up with the same ideas.
2. There was no qualifier on the payoff--it didn't seem to matter how an idea impacted the business because employees still got rewarded equally with dinner certificate or movie tickets.
3. At first the PIP coordinator had too many ideas to deal with, and there was no feedback about what happened to the ideas. Employees were rewarded for just coming up with the ideas.

In the long run the whole program slowly disintegrated through apathy. Then we went to a Crosby Quality seminar and completely revamped the program. That's when I started working here. The new system was called Error Cause Removal (ECR) and was focused on resolving chronic problems. Based on our seminar we decided to eliminate all incentives and just make the ECR part of the job. It sounded great in theory, so we asked the supervisors to administer the program.

However, we did have some problems:

1. Employees really resented not having any incentives--so many didn't participate --these "stupid" little rewards were part of the culture.
2. The employees who did participate developed a "we bitch, you fix" attitude-- they didn't feel like they had to do anything to implement their ideas.

3. Supervisors felt overwhelmed with the new responsibility and many never acted on the ideas; they never bought into the program; few employees received feedback about their ideas.
4. It was a paperwork disaster--the amount of documentation required and the level of detail was overwhelming to everyone.

These are the lessons I've taken from these incidents:

1. We need to respond to people and their ideas.
2. It has to be a simple program.
3. It needs to empower employees to work on the solutions.
4. Adminstrators need to want to do it.
5. There needs to be some kind of incentive.

Our new program is called Novel Ideas For the Future (NIFF) and will be based on the following items:

1. We will provide training for the departments involved in the program. The training will include: problem-solving skills, plant systems for getting work done, etc.
2. Every employee will receive a response within 72 hours of his or her suggestion, with a response that says either:
   • no
   • yes, we'll do it immediately
   • yes, we'll do it when we are able
3. The incentives will be based on the number of ideas: if an employee has 10 ideas he or she will get a flashlight, 25 ideas will get a dinner for two (whether or not the idea is implemented).

This is the sketch of the NIFF program so far. What I want to know is:

1. Have we analyzed the problems effectively?
2. Are we proceeding correctly?
3. What should we be doing?

Objectives:
1. Specify the precise response you would make to the manager.
2. Specify the approach you would use in presenting your reactions.
3. Provide the rationale for the approach and proposal.

Case 9.2: Finding the "Success Formula" for Innovation

Purpose: To understand the major roadblocks in the innovation process.

Situation: The CEO of a company has just commissioned a study of innovations that have "worked" in the organization. He exclaims:

> I just finished reading the chapter on innovation in *Communicating for Managerial Effectiveness*. It helped me pinpoint one of my deepest frustrations about this organization:
>
> There are far too many ideas that never make it to the implementation stage. I want to know why. I can't seem to figure it out. We've got good people here. What I'd like you to do is research three cases in which innovations have "failed" for some reason and three cases in which the innovations have been successfully implemented. I want you to interview or document each case so that we have some rich historical background on each situation. I'll leave it to you to define success or failure. Based on these six cases, I'd like you to give me 10 specific guidelines about how to improve the innovative climate at this organization. My new motto is going to be, "Innovate or Stagnate." But I need more than a slogan to motivate the employees. The book provides a good **general** background but what I need are specifics about our company. That is why I'm so intent on having well-documented cases. Then we can extrapolate from these situations the precise nature of the problems we are encountering. You might want to take a careful look at the notion of "diffusion of innovation" (pp. 195-196) because it may be tied up in this problem as well. Maybe it has something to do with our problems.

Objectives:

1. Using an organization with which you are familiar,
   a. identify three successful innovations that have been implemented
   b. identify three innovations that have failed
   c. explain the reasons for the above successes or failures
   d. create a list of "10 guidelines to improve the innovative climate" in an organization
2. Specify the approach you would use in presenting your results to the CEO.
3. Provide your rationale for the approach and the research findings.

Chapter 10: Communication Ethics

Chapter Summary

It is only recently that the subject of corporate ethics has been addressed. The reasons for this are varied. One explanation is that our heritage seeks to give people the widest possible freedom and individual discretion in forming moral opinions. There is the thought that discussing ethics will lead to imposing one's morality on others. In addition, ethical discussions are avoided because they are seen as irrelevant to the fundamental purpose of business, namely making a profit or increasing shareholder wealth.

This chapter addresses many ethical dilemmas facing the manager, such as whistle-blowing, leaks, rumors, and gossip. While there is no guarantee that a corporation or its employees will behave ethically, this chapter suggests a model of the "ethical organization." An organization, striving for ethical behavior, will integrate individuals of personal integrity in an organizational culture of strong principles, governed by organizational policies that support the principles. There are three critical ethical policy issues that the organization must face:

1. *what information should be gathered to assist in making decisions?*
2. *how should the information be gathered?*
3. *how should the information be used?*

Learning Objectives

After studying this chapter, you will be able to:

- discuss the ethical dilemmas facing the manager

- describe what makes an ethical organization

- determine the primary policy issues facing the corporation

- identify the dilemmas in gathering information

Key Terms and Concepts

corporate social responsibility   p. 264
trade secrets   p. 268

Chapter Outline

I. Foundation
   A. Reasons why discussion of communication ethics has been previously
      avoided
      1. Seen as imposing one's morality on others
      2. Viewed as irrelevant to main purpose of business
      3. "It depends" philosophy
   B. Fundamental assumptions of discussions on ethics
      1. Every communication decision has an ethical
         dimension to it
      2. Communication ethics involves motives and impacts
      3. Ethical nature of communication must be considered
         within the context of "who, what, when,and where"

II. Ethical dilemmas
   A. Secrecy
   B. Whistle-blowing
   C. Leaks
   D. Rumors and gossip
   E. Lying
   F. Euphemisms
   G. Ambiguity
   H. Apology

III. The "Ethical Organization": A strategic approach to corporate ethics involves the integration of:
   A. Corporate culture
   B. Organizational policy
      1. Policy issue 1: What information should be gathered?
      2. Policy issue 2: How is information gathered?
      3. Policy issue 3: How is the information used?
   C. Individual character
      1. Discretion
      2. Relevancy
      3. Accuracy
      4. Fairness
      5. Proper timing

Exercise 10.1: Identifying Ethical Dilemmas

Match the following examples with the ethical dilemmas they describe:

    a. lying
    b. ambiguity
    c. gossip
    d. rumors
    e. euphemisms
    f. leaks
    g. secrecy
    h. whistle-blowing

_____ 1. using the term "passed away" instead of "died"

_____ 2. an employee goes public with information about safety abuses in the organization

_____ 3. an employee anonymously passes on information to his supervisor that another worker is selling corporate secrets to a competitor

_____ 4. a manager responds vaguely to an employee's request for a raise by stating, "Have patience, we have plans for you."

_____ 5. an employee transmits information about an unconfirmed report of a corporate takeover

_____ 6. an employee calls in to work to report a "sick day" in order to have an extended weekend

_____ 7. a CEO decides to tell only her executive committee about plans for building a major new plant in order to avoid compromising the project

Exercise 10.2: Creating an Ethical Organization

The book discusses three basic components of an ethical organization:

- Corporate Culture (CC)

- Individual Responsibility (IR)

- Organizational Policy (OP)

Which component most accurately describes the strategy underlying the following corporate activities? Use the abbreviations above to indicate your choice.

_____ 1. In the annual address to employees, the CEO makes a commitment to "corporate due process."

_____ 2. The organization revises its procedures for selling the corporation's "mailing lists" to other companies.

_____ 3. The organization sets up training courses for employees about maintaining personal standards of ethical communication when interacting with co-workers and clients.

_____ 4. A statement is placed in the corporate philosophy about the organization's commitment to the ethical use of information.

_____ 5. In selection interviews, all prospective employees are asked about how they would handle a case of employee theft.

_____ 6. In orientation sessions for new employees, the issue of corporate social responsibility is discussed.

_____ 7. A company creates a task force to evaluate the necessity of routinely collecting certain information about clients.

Exercise 10.3: Making Ethical Choices

In each of the following situations determine (1) what major ethical issues are at stake, (2) if the person behaved ethically, and (3) why or why not.

1. An employee tells a colleague that he thinks his manager is about to "get the ax" because of some financial irregularities in the departmental books.

2. While at a cocktail party, a salesperson overhears a marketing representative from a competitor describe a new product and pricing scheme. The next day the salesperson passes along the information to his company's marketing department.

3. An executive has to make the "toughest decision of his life" and choose between two equally qualified top flight managers to be vice president of a new division. While culling through the personnel files one final time, he notices that manager A has had a history of heart problems although he has never missed a day of work. The executive decides on manager B.

4. A salesperson realizes that in order to make the sale, he will have to promise an earlier delivery date than his competition. He finds out that his company cannot possibly meet the earlier date. Nevertheless, he promises the earlier date in order to close the sale, hoping something can be worked out.

5. A top executive committee discovers that one of their products, in unusual circumstances, can cause injury. Measures are taken in the current production procedures to alleviate the problems. However, after computing the costs and benefits they decide against a recall and choose to stonewall any investigations, hoping to settle any lawsuits quietly out of court.

Exercise 10.4: Evaluating an Apology

The general manager of large hotel in Chicago was talking to one of his supervisors on Monday afternoon. In the course of his conversation he used a number of racial slurs and sexual stereotypes to describe "the help." An employee testing a wireless microphone for a seminar that night had inadvertently left it in the manager's office in the "on" position. About 50 employees setting up for a banquet in an adjacent room were startled to hear their manager over the speaker system. When they heard him use this offensive language they were outraged. Of course, the manager knew nothing about this until he was confronted by some very angry members of the union. The next day he issued the following written memo.

Tuesday

To: All Staff
From: GM

Yesterday, some employees inadvertently overheard part of a private conversation because a careless employee left a wireless microphone in my private office. My remarks were made in a confidential setting and my comments were not intended to offend anyone. I want to apologize if anyone was hurt by my remarks. Let me assure you that I regard everyone at the Hotel as a valued part of the team.

Evaluate this apology in terms of the principles discussed in the chapter. Provide suggestions for improvement.

Exercise 10.5: Thought Quote

The author of the textbook concludes chapter 10 with the following remarks:

> One feels a tremendous obligation to not make a mockery of such sacrifice, to not abuse the freedom but use it to pursue the very best in life. We often hear of the freedom of speech, but here on that hot humid day in Washington, D.C. I thought about the responsibilities of speech.

What "speech responsibilities" are you personally committed to? Identify six examples.

Case 10.1: Communication During Downsizing

Purpose: To develop an action plan for communicating a difficult message in an ethical manner.

Situation:

1. You are the communication advisor to the head administrator of a major hospital in your local area. She asked you to develop a procedure for informing employees and the community about an impending layoff of 200 employees on January 15.

2. The administrator wants you to devise a plan that minimizes the amount of tension, friction, and "down time" in the workplace. Moreover, she wants you to include provisions for coping with difficulties after an announcement of the layoff has been made.

3. The hospital employs about 1,500 workers and the layoff was the last-resort measure to put the organization in the black. The people who will be laid off will be from a cross-section of the organization and include both employees and management.

4. The administrator has given you $65,000 for any related expenses that may be incurred in meeting her objectives.

Methods:

1. Describe your precise plan both on a strategic and tactical level.

2. Justify the strategic and tactical decisions you are proposing.

3. Discuss how you will present your plan to the head administrator.

Case 10.2: The Ethical Use of Information

Purpose: To create a training program that motivates employees to use information ethically.

Situation: You have been hired by the training department of a major bank to develop a 3-hour seminar for new employees about how to treat customer information. The training director directs you as follows:

> Because of the nature of our business we have a lot of temporary employees in teller positions. They usually are young and have just a high school education. We've had several incidents in the last few months in which customer information has been inadvertently released to unauthorized personnel. In our orientation sessions we share with new employees the guidelines about confidentiality. But maybe the guidelines are too difficult to understand. However, my feeling is that the employees understand the guidelines but become careless. They may forget them, since there are so many things for a new employee to remember. I think the **underlying** problem is that our training is focused on the head and not the heart. I mean, we tell them the policy but we don't motivate them to comply. They don't really feel the importance of the issue. What they need to feel is that a violation of policy can damage our reputation for "customer-focused service." We really don't underscore the consequences for the customer if we don't treat information properly.
>
> I'd like your training program to include the policy issues but go beyond the basics. These employees need to be motivated to treat information in ways they never have in the past. Most of these employees have grown up in a society that treats information like air--it's like information is there for everybody to have. We can't afford to have that ethic in our bank.
>
> Therefore, I'd like you to prepare an outline of specific goals, content, and exercises that you would have for such a seminar.

Method:

1. Conduct background research on the information policies of a local bank.
2. Develop a training program for the bank.
3. Provide a rationale for the program on a strategic and tactical level.
4. Provide a rationale for how you would present your proposal to this training director.

103

References

Armstrong, D. (1992). *Managing by Storying Around: A New Method of Leadership.* New York: Doubleday.

Beer, M. (1988). Performance appraisal: Dilemmas and possibilities. In AMA (Ed.), *Organizational dynamics special reports: Performance appraisal* (pp. 15-27). New York: AMA.

Blanchard, K., & Johnson, S. (1982). *The one minute manager.* New York: Berkley.

De Meyer, A. (1991). Tech talk: How managers are stimulating global R & D communication. *Sloan Management Review,* 32(3), 49-66.

De Mille, A. (1991). *Martha: The life and work of Martha Graham.* New York: Random House.

Midgely, M. (1989). *Wisdom, information, & wonder: What is knowledge for?* London: Routledge.

Petroski, H. (1992). *The Pencil: A history of design and circumstance.* New York: Knopf.

Rummler, G., & Brache, A. (1991). *Improving performance: How to managage the white space on the organizational chart.* San Francisco: Jossey-Bass.

Shaprio, B., Rangan, V., & Sviokla, J. (July-August 1992). Staple yourself to an order. *Harvard Business Review,* 70(40), 113-122.

Welch, J. (1993, January 25). Jack Welch's lessons for success. *Fortune,* pp. 86-93.

Wheeler, J. (1992). Black Holes. In S. Hawking (Ed), *Stephen Hawking's a brief history of time: A reader's companion* (pp.85-86). New York: Bantam.

Answers

Exercise 1.1

1. c   2. a   3. d   4. a   5. d   6. c   7. a   8. a   9. c   10. d

Exercise 1.2

1. r   2. r   3. i   4. i   5. i   6. i   7. r

Exercise 1.3

1. a   2. a   3. c   4. d   5. a   6. c   7. c   8. d   9. c   10. d

Exercise 2.1

1.   2. ✔   3.   4. ✔   5. ✔   6. ✔   7.   8.   9.   10. ✔

Exercise 2.2

There are a variety of answers for this question but here are some ideas.
a. color, not ripe, golfing, money, naive
b. person's name, carrying something to the limit; top performance, burnt out
c. secret writing, a set of ethical rules, a set of engineering plans, translating ideas into a message

Exercise 2.3

There are numerous acceptable answers for this exercise, we have just identified some of them.

a. the subject matter involves classroom performance; the professor is in a position to know about the student's level of performance; the conversation focuses on performance in a recent class rather than an overall appraisal of the student's abilities

b. the subject matter involves the employee's performance; the employee's performance is linked to the department's monthly sales figures; the boss is in a position to judge the employee's performance; the employee's performance can be judged separately from the department's performance

c. the subject could involve the employee's perception of the supervisor's performance; the employee has access to information to judge the supervisor's performance; the place of the conversation may imply that the supervisor wants only positive information; the scope of the performance to be judged involves the recent past, not the entire career of the supervisor; the employee is in a position to judge the supervisor

d. the subject could involve the boyfriend's social skills in a party setting; the time frame involves events during the mixer; the girlfriend is in a position to make a judgment about the boyfriend's social skills

Exercise 2.4

There are a variety of acceptable answers but here are some suggestions.

1. PM - introduction of one party to another; SM - The use of Dr. and Mrs. implies a relationship of superior to inferior; the person making the introduction feels that a physician is more important than a college professor

2. PM - the candidate wants to create economic opportunities; SM - The use of the phrase "you people" may imply a status difference between the candidate and the group; the minority group has accepted handouts in the past.

3. PM - the manager will no longer receive the report; SM - CEO may feel the manager is no longer important enough to receive this report; since the message is in a written form, the decision is final

Exercise 3.1

a "We"   b. "I "   c. "It" but ultimately impacts "Them"   d. "I" with some impact on "We"
e. "Them"   f. "Them"   g. "It" but ultimately impacts "Them"

Exercise 3.2

a. allows for change, links to an ennobling vision, inspires creativity   b. not confined to a certain type of product, inspiring vision, provides a meaningful purpose for employees

Exercise 3.3

	Arrow	Circuit	Dance
I	• Only the tough survive	• We want employees who communicate and work well with others	• We value employees who are effective communicators as well as have technical competence
We	• The chain-of-command is what is really important	• Everyone is treated equally	• Project-oriented teams inspire teamwork and quality performance
Them	• Customers will be satisfied if we do our job right	• Customers are our partners for creating a better tomorrow	• We must not only satisfy our customers, we must anticipate their needs, as well
It	• We make the best products	• As long as our customer is satisfied, we are satisfied	• We must not only meet our own tough standards but our customers, as well

Exercise 4.1

a. 5 b. 4 c. 1 d. 3 e. 2

Exercise 4.2

a. 5 b. 1 c. 2 d. 3 e. 4

Exercise 4.3

1. UI   2. PI   3. KI   4. AI   5. UI   6. AI   7. UI
8. employee level KI; organizational level UI

Exercise 4.4

Data: transforming inklings into measurable units
Information: transforming data into an organized and meaningful form
Knowledge: transforming information into understanding
Empowerment: transforming knowledge into action

Advantages
• The variety in the density of the background at different stages shows an abundance of data versus information, versus knowledge, versus empowerment
• Triangle shows how data combines to make information, how information combines to create knowledge
• The different shape of the circle and triangle indicates the fundamental differences between organizational processes and goals

Disadvantages
• Too linear, doesn't show feedback loops
• Doesn't show processes before the creation of data
• Doesn't show other impacts on organizational goals

Exercise 5.1

2, 3, 1, 4, 5

Exercise 5.2

4, 3, 5, 2, 1

Exercise 5.3

+	−
1. group meeting	memo
2. voicE-mail	bulletin board
3. bulletin board	video conference
4. publication or memo	voice mail
5. publication or videotape	face-to-face

Exercise 6.1

1. T   2. F   3. F   4. F   5. F   6. F   7. F   8. T   9. T   10. F   11. T   12. F

Exercise 6.2

1. S   2. IF   3. JR   4. S   5. FF   6. S   7. IF

Exercise 6.3

1. I want to thank you for working overtime on this project. (reinforcement of behavior) This is the kind of **dedication** we value in our organization. (link to character quality)

2. Your new idea for processing bills is fantastic. (reinforcement of behavior) It really demonstrates your **creativity** and commitment to our corporate goal of providing "cost effective service." (link to character quality and organizational goals)

3. I want to complement you on how you implemented the new system in your department. (reinforcement of behavior) You overcame many actual and potential problems. Your **persistence** is the perfect model for other employees. (link to character quality)

Exercise 7.1

a. E   b. M   c. E   d. I   e. M

Exercise 7.2

a. B   b. AC   c. A   d. D

e. A   f. DP   g. A   h. D

Exercise 7-3

	Routine Change	Moderate Change	Large-Scale Change
a. Need for a dynamic channel	L	M	H
b. Need to discourage receiver from asking a lot of questions	H	M	L
c. Need for persuasive appeals	L	M	H
d. Need for highly credible channels	H	H	H
e. Need to economize language through jargon	H	M	L
f. Need to reduce the number of channels used to communicate	H	M	L
g. Need to standardize information display	H	M	L
h. Need to "contextualize" information in terms of organizational vision	L	M	H

	Routine Change	Moderate Change	Large-Scale Change
i. Probability of resistance	L	M	H
j. Probability of rumors	L	M	H
k. Likelihood sender will know receiver's information needs	H	M	L
l. Likelihood that interpersonal relationships will become a resistance point	L	M	H

108

Exercise 7.4

1. When the sender knows the information needs of receivers, there is less need for redundancy in channels. Receivers learn to expect certain information in certain places and it wastes organizational time and effort to supply it in other formats. If employees know that the work schedule is posted every week by the time clock, there is little need to post that information elsewhere or through other channels. Routine information should be displayed in a minimum number of channels.

2. More standardized forms of communication need to be used when announcing routine changes in order to allow employees to access the information quickly and effectively. The very act of using nonstandard forms of information display may send a powerful secondary message about the willingness of management to ease the transition into a major change, thereby minimizing the resistance the change.

3. The larger the change, the greater the likelihood of resistance. With major changes, the unique employee concerns need to be addressed. However, the more routine the change is, the less need there is to encourage questions. In fact, allowing too many questions about routine changes can waste precious organizational resources and create a climate difficult to implement larger scale changes. Unlike the Circuit manager's orientation, encouraging more questions can actually be debilitating when dealing with routine change.

4. Jargon can be an effective way to economically transmit a lot of information in a routine change situation. When the change is more nonroutine, dynamic channels are needed. Jargon may encourage misunderstandings and discourage question asking by employees. They may feel "dumb" for asking for clarification of terms and this obviates the power of a dynamic channel.

5. Contextualizing information is a way to persuade employees. It provides a method for employees to interpret the large-scale changes occurring. Contextualizing is not as necessary for more routine information, such as announcing the company's softball team schedule.

Exercise 8.1

a. 21, 28   b. 36, 9

The formula for this problem is as follows:

$$\frac{n!}{(n-2)!\,2} = \text{Number of Comm. Links}$$

* n = number of departments

Exercise 8.2

a. job rotation   b. job switching   c. brainstorming

Exercise 8.3

a. C   b. A   c. C   d. A   e. D   f. A   g. A   h. A, C, or D depending on rationale

i. A   j. D   k. D   l. A   m. D

Exercise 9.1

Stage	Evaluation criteria	Critical questions
Idea Generation	novelty	Is the idea unique or unusual?
Feasibility Analysis	possibility	Can the idea work?
Reality Testing	practicality	Does the idea fit with organizational objectives?
Implementation	activity	Has the idea been acted on?

Exercise 9.2

1. b   2. d   3. a   4. c   5. a   6. d   7. b

Exercise 9-3

1. a   2. d   3. c   4. b   5. a

Exercise 9.4

	Idea Generation	Feasibility Analysis	Reality Testing	Implementation
Face-to-Face	✔	✔	✔	✔
Telephone			✔	✔
Formal Presentation			✔	✔
Memos				✔
Fax			✔	✔
E-mail	✔	✔		
Computer Conference	✔	✔		
Bulletin Board				✔
Voice Mail			✔	✔
Teleconference			✔	✔
Group Meeting	✔		✔	✔
Video Conference			✔	✔

Exercise 9.5

Many of our "answers" for Exercise 9.4 are contingent on the type of innovation and scope of change required. For instance, for some minor change a bulletin board would work out well in the implementation phase but if the change is major then a more dynamic channel, like a group meeting or video conference, might be called for.

The basic notion behind Exercises 9.4 and 9.5 is to have you understand some underlying issues regarding how channel choice can impact the innovation process. For instance, in the idea generation stage it is important to have a lot of give-and-take, like in a group meeting . If possible it is also important to remove corporate "political issues" from the agenda, so as to clear the way for fresh and novel ideas. E-mail and computer conferences are helpful in this endeavor. On the other hand, when it comes to the implementation part of the process, there is often a need to grapple with the corporate "political realities." In this phase, more robust channels like video conferences or group meetings allow employees to "buy in" to major changes. You'll also probably notice that the majority of the channels used in organizations seem to be most fully compatible with reality testing and implementation rather than idea generation and feasibility analysis. Perhaps this is why changes are slow in coming for many organizations. There are other underlying issues inherent in these exercises. We have just given you a hint at some of the larger issues.

Exercise 9.6

1. Offer sizable financial rewards for new ideas
2. Stick to regulations
3. Approve a lot of ideas that don't get implemented
4. Use a suggestion box
5. Discourage experimentation
6. Respond to suggestions slowly
7. Insist on detailed justifications for new ideas
8. Discourage interdepartmental communication
9. Only reward employees who have ideas that "pan out"
10. Discourage diversity

Exercise 10.1

1. e   2. h   3. f   4. b   5. d   6. a   7. g

Exercise 10.2

1. CC   2. OP   3. IR   4. CC   5. IR or OP   6. CC   7. OP

Exercise 10.3

1. Gossip, fairness   2. Rumors, secrets, discretion   3. Information use, relevancy
4. Lying, accuracy   5. Secrets, fairness, whistle-blowing

Exercise 10.4

Issues include: timing, personal responsibility, relevancy standard, brevity of message, and how the GM will respond in the future.